# Scattered Thoughts

From His Word to My Mind

# Scattered Thoughts

From His Word to My Mind

Oregean Adams

# Copyright

©2018 by Oregean Adams. All rights reserved.

No part of this book may be reproduced in any written, electronic, recording, or photocopying without written permission of the publisher or author. The exception would be in the case of brief quotations embodied in the critical articles or reviews and pages where permission is specifically granted by the publisher or author.

Holy Bible Scriptures found in NIV, KJV, NKJV and CEV.

Books may be purchased by contacting the publisher or the author.

Cover Design: Ministering Moments
Publisher: Butterfly Typeface Publishing, Little Rock AR
Editor: Ingrid Zacharias

ISBN: 978-1-947656-52-9
ISBN10: 194765652x

1. Religion 2. Inspirational 3. Spirituality

First Edition
Printed in the United States

# Dedication

Inspired by the Holy Ghost, written for you!

"Now to Him who is able to do exceedingly abundantly above all that we ask or think, according to the power that works in us, to Him be glory in the church by Christ Jesus to all generations, forever and ever. Amen."

Ephesians 3:20-21 NKJV

## Table of Contents

Preface .................................................................................. 21

Watch What You Say............................................................ 23

Relationships........................................................................ 25

Forgive Them ....................................................................... 27

How to Endure the Cross ..................................................... 29

The God of the Valley .......................................................... 31

It Is Finished ........................................................................ 33

Over Coming The Obedience Obstacle ............................... 35

How To Get Over It .............................................................. 37

Getting To The Hem ............................................................ 40

Out Of The Box Praise ......................................................... 42

Set Up for A Miracle ............................................................ 44

I'm Still Here ........................................................................ 46

A Sin In A Mercy Situation ................................................... 48

Dealing With The Devil ....................................................... 50

Dealing With The Devil Round Two .................................... 52

The Bush That Burns ........................................................... 54

Did You Forget To Say Thanks? ........................................... 56

Do Not Play With God ......................................................... 58

God's Word Benefits Us ...................................................... 60

The Power Is In The Command ........................................... 62

You Can Make It .................................................................. 64

The Gospel Says You Can Be Saved .................................... 66

When You Feel Like Giving Up ............................................ 68

His Will Be Done .................................................................. 70

Jesus Wisdom ........................................................................ 72
Good Things Bad Boy ......................................................... 74
When Jesus Is Inside ........................................................... 76
What Made Them Wise Men? ........................................... 78
Blessings Are Plenty ........................................................... 80
What Did Jesus See? ........................................................... 82
The Life ................................................................................. 84
How To Recover .................................................................. 86
I Made It Through The Night ........................................... 88
Not Bowing Down .............................................................. 90
Saul's Damascus Road Experience ................................... 92
What Gate Are You At? ...................................................... 94
Loving My Enemies ............................................................ 96
What Prayer Does For Me .................................................. 98
Are You Teachable? ...........................................................100
Is God Ever Too Late? .......................................................102
She Came Crooked But She Left Straight ......................104
Can You Say Yes Again? ...................................................106
Job's Shoes ..........................................................................108
God Will Provide ...............................................................110
Do It God's Way .................................................................112
Battling For My Blessing ..................................................114
Men and Women Trying To Do It Their Way ...............116
They Stood Together ........................................................118
What Made Him So Blessed ............................................120
How To Overcome Fear ....................................................122
How To Deal With Pain ....................................................124

| | |
|---|---|
| How To Treat Jesus | 126 |
| Your Needs Are Always Met | 128 |
| What Makes You Sing? | 130 |
| There Is A Need | 132 |
| What's Wrong Worshiper? | 134 |
| The Church | 136 |
| A Salty Church | 138 |
| First Love Forgotten | 140 |
| Let God Be God | 142 |
| Good Attitude No Matter What | 144 |
| The Lord's Priorities | 146 |
| Are You Standing? | 148 |
| I AM WHO I AM | 150 |
| False Advertisement | 152 |
| Just A Reminder | 154 |
| Great Cloud Of Witnesses | 156 |
| I Still Remember | 158 |
| Let The Word Work In You | 160 |
| Don't Wait Until You Are In Hell To Get It Right | 162 |
| Too Sleepy To Pray | 164 |
| Lost But Still Valuable | 166 |
| Good Recipe For Wisdom | 168 |
| Leaving Better | 170 |
| Putting The Word Into Action | 172 |
| The Other Side Of Midnight | 174 |
| The Purpose Of The Word | 176 |
| Do It | 178 |

| | |
|---|---|
| The Sanctuary | 180 |
| Our Job | 182 |
| Balanced In Your Belief | 184 |
| Don't Mistake Delay For Denial | 186 |
| Don't Lose Your Fire | 188 |
| Prescription For A New Healthy Church | 190 |
| I Have Got Somewhere To Be | 192 |
| How Much Do I Owe Him? | 194 |
| Do You Want To Get Well? | 196 |
| There Is A War Going On | 198 |
| No Weapon Formed Will Prosper | 200 |
| Saul Lost It | 202 |
| Thanksgiving | 204 |
| Still Standing | 206 |
| Friday The Thirteenth | 208 |
| My Blessings Are Chasing Me | 210 |
| Hold On | 212 |
| Don't Let The Devil Get In You | 214 |
| The Power Of Giving | 216 |
| Use It Or Lose It | 218 |
| When You've Had Enough | 220 |
| Lessons From The Cross | 222 |
| Now I See | 224 |
| Faith Beyond The Facts | 226 |
| Life For A Dead Situation | 228 |
| Is God Worth Ten Cent? | 230 |
| From A Member To A Worker | 232 |

No One Is Good Enough To Go To Heaven ..................... 234
A Good Example To Follow ..................................... 236
Don't Go Home The Same Way You Came ..................... 238
Keep Hope Alive ............................................... 240
God Sent Him ................................................. 242
Winning Over Worry ........................................... 244
The Order Of Service .......................................... 246
Who Has The Best View? ....................................... 248
Children Changed By A Touch ................................ 250
It's Your Season .............................................. 252
Let It Go ..................................................... 254
Being A Friend ............................................... 256
Destined For Destruction ..................................... 258
He Is Our Amazing Grace (John 1:14) ........................ 260
He Gets The Credit ........................................... 262
The Trinity .................................................. 264
Joy Comes In The Morning .................................... 266
A Good Day To Obey .......................................... 268
Oneness With God ............................................ 270
Mother To Son ............................................... 272
You Are Not As Smart As You Think You Are ................. 274
Who Are You Helping? ........................................ 276
Praise God For His Love ...................................... 278
Real True Praise ............................................. 280
Prayer Answered ............................................. 282
In Him Only .................................................. 284
Jesus Christ Master Teacher .................................. 286

Everything Belongs To God..................................................288
Do You Believe The Good News ............................................290
A Wise Word To The Young...................................................292
The Vision................................................................................294
We Are No Secret To The Lord..............................................296
Connected To The Right Person............................................298
When Jesus Does It................................................................300
God's Family ...........................................................................302
What Is Your Mind Set On?....................................................304
Natural Desires vs. Spiritual Desires ...................................306
Most Gracious ........................................................................308
The Day The World Got A Major Overhaul.......................310
The Gift That Just Keeps On Giving.....................................312
Your Time Is Running Out ....................................................314
Take It Up With God ..............................................................316
No Shame................................................................................318
Admonished to Love Everyone ............................................320
Whole Again ..........................................................................322
It's Not Your Business ...........................................................325
A Blessed Nation....................................................................327
Anger Management ..............................................................329
Who Is My Family?.................................................................331
The Church Belongs To God.................................................333
So Impatient ...........................................................................335
Is Your Flesh Burning?...........................................................337
Work It Out .............................................................................339
Brotherly Love........................................................................341

| | |
|---|---|
| A Good Wife | 343 |
| You Have Been Divinely Appointed | 345 |
| Family Reunion | 347 |
| Great Men Of Service | 349 |
| The Voice Of God | 351 |
| What Would Be Your *Proper Place*? | 353 |
| Confinement | 355 |
| Spiritual Adultery | 357 |
| They Say | 359 |
| A Three-Fold Cord | 361 |
| A Broken Spirit | 363 |
| The Promise Of Forgiveness | 365 |
| Will You Ever Learn? | 367 |
| The Light | 369 |
| The Christian Minister | 371 |
| Music Creates A Memory | 373 |
| Just Look | 376 |
| Armor Bearer | 378 |
| Pay What You Owe | 380 |
| The Big "O's" | 382 |
| I Found Him | 385 |
| What Are You Speaking? | 387 |
| Faith Based On Experience | 389 |
| Every Where You Go He Has Already Been | 391 |
| About the Author | 393 |

**Also by Oregean Adams**

Scattered Thoughts (Volume II)
*More Words From Him To Me And You*

# Foreword

My relationship with Christ is something that I've never taken lightly. I've always attended church service, been an active member in ministry, and made sure that I wasn't just walking around carrying the title "Christian". It is my consistent goal to become closer to Christ. You know... a truly intimate relationship. A relationship that not only involves him knowing all about me and having a daily yearning to spend time with me, but one where I share the exact same feelings. However, this has not only been a goal of mine, but also a struggle.

Throughout my adult life, I've unintentionally found myself often letting life and all that comes along with it get in the way of developing that genuine rock-solid relationship with Christ. After having the opportunity to read *Scattered Thoughts*, I have been impacted tremendously! Not only has it pushed me to want to learn and grow more in my studies of God's Word, but it's made it a lot easier! I was so frustrated with books and articles I'd tried reading in the past that never help and often only confused me even more. Oregean Adams, however writes and discusses topics in a way that anyone could follow!

I truly believe that she is God ordained and destined to be a blessing to the people of God by sharing her wisdom and knowledge of his word, not only through what she has read and been taught but definitely based on her experiences. I'm blessed to know her first as my mother, secondly as my friend, and now as a great author! I trust that her writings will be a blessing to each and every one that picks it up and reads it.

Congratulations and Many Blessings to you Mommy!

Love Always,


Chelsea B. Adams, M.S.

# Acknowledgments

I also want to thank my Family for the Love that we share beginning with my husband Mitchell B. Adams, words cannot express how much I appreciate you.

To my children Helen L. Leniear, Pamela D. Ferrell, Kerry L. Ferrell, and Chelsea B. Adams; I love you dearly... I share this book with you. It is a great honor to be called Mama by you. It is also a great honor to have been chosen by Almighty God (EL SHADDAI) to do this great work.

I pray and thank God for all of you daily, along with my beautiful grand children: and for all of my other family members who are too numerous to name. God bless,

To Be Continued...

# Preface

"And the Lord said too me, your Latter shall be greater (Haggai 2:9)."

This Book is dedicated to my beloved Pastor, Eric L. Alexander for his awesome teaching and preaching ability, and for his boldness in speaking the gospel of Our Lord and Savior, "Jesus Christ".

A part of the name of this book is also through the inspiration of my Pastor.

This Book has been created to help you in your daily walk with God. Step into its pages and let it take hold of you. You can read it daily, or you can read it all at once. But let the Holy Spirit guide you as you read, and go through the Scriptures, believe me *He* is here.

## Watch What You Say

(Judges 12:5-6)

It will come back to you

Say what, the tongue is speaking when it ought to be still; and when it ought to talk it says nothing.

Something happens when you start winning in life. People get jealous, mad, crazy, etc. Just because you are doing well they don't understand. But greater is He that is in me than he that is in the world.

Watch people when you get ready to cross over. You could not tell in their case who was who. We should not front because all it does is gets us into trouble.

It's not enough to look like a Christian because soon your mouth is going to tell on you. Profanity you say I got it from my parents.

You gossip and pick up a bad dialect; you know everybody's business.

You can tell who you are by how you talk.

Do you belong to the Lord or the adversary the devil?

You say the same things that the sinners say.

You are no holier than your tongue. If your tongue is dirty your heart is dirty (Matthew. 12:3) out of the abundance of your heart you speak. What is in you is coming up and it is coming out. Your mouth will determine your destiny. Talk up and watch your life.

God has programmed our bodies to watch what our tongue says (Proverbs 18:21). The power of life and death is in the tongue. We quickly say call me, because we do not know how to say no. Not knowing how to say no will get you in trouble. One word can get you out. Just say mercy Jesus, demons tremble at the name of Jesus.

Are you putting your mouth on others? Well your mouth is really not the issue. God has fixed it so your mouth will tell on you. There is a place in your life where people cannot even fake. (Psalms 51:10) speaks of a clean heart.

We speak things on our self. Your body hears and goes in that direction, oh my. For instance I am not sick but I am well. I'm blessed. Their mouth held them up.

You need to commission your mouth to speak holy, if you don't believe just go on. If your mouth can't say it; then you can't achieve it, being on the top of the mountain requires that I trust God because as sure as I go up I will come back down.

Does your life look just like your speech? If you read the lesson scripture you will find that they said one word. But it was the wrong one word and resulted in the loss of their life. The word they said was sibbolleth, which is not real but faking and shaking. The word they should have said was shibboleth, which means I go with God. Watch what you say.

# Relationships

(St. Luke 15:17)

It's what you make it.

A parable is an earthly story with a heavenly meaning.

Jesus said; how can you say you love me who you have never seen yet you hate your brother who you see daily.

It is time to let go of the hate and not caring for one another. This "I" thing gets in the way of a person living a holy life. Some people do not let things like this bother them. Simply because it is not about them, some people tend to think the way they feel, that the sun rises and sets with them; they feel that folks owe them something.

A part of life is to pay your dues watch who you connect yourself with. Because anywhere away from the Father is a far country.

Check your connections because there is a transfer of spirit. People drop God's Word and try to handle things themselves. Connections affect your appetite. He was hungry he was willing to try something he normally would not have done. Example: How did I get here? Hanging with the wrong person will mess you up.

Even though he was starving there was something he just would not do. It should be the same with us today. You need to know that God will starve your old man out. You need to tell your old man that I am going to fast and hurry up and kill you.

Don't change your rules don't lower your standards. In a few days you will keel over and die to the flesh.

Don't become a professional sinner, do a self-evaluation, learn how to talk to yourself, make a decision to get over it. How do I do this? Just let it go.

Don't make excuses admit when you are wrong. A good person is a person who knows when they are wrong.

Heaven takes it personal when you are at odds with another person. The way I know you love me is when you love your neighbor.

When you are wrong, go back and say I'm sorry.

Be very careful of folks asking about other folks business.

God will bless you to work with what you have. The prodigal son had to pay for his praise, I had to pay for my praise, and you my friend have to do the same.

# Forgive Them

(St. Luke 23:33-34)

Jesus really is an Awesome Savior

Have you ever acted out of character? Forgive them is easier said than done. Forgiveness is dismissing a debt, releasing a demand, releasing the consequences, releasing your thoughts to the offender.

When you forgive you give up your right to be mad or get even. We don't just get mad at the deed, but we get mad because we can't get the person back. Then you are holding on to the sin. Let it go! When you forgive you free yourself.

Don't you die in bondage waiting on someone else to be the first to move?

Forgiveness is between you and God. You gave up your right to dwell on it when you gave your life to Christ. But every now and then you want to bring it back up because you want to handle things yourself.

We must extend mercy and grace. The more you don't forgive, the more you carry others. Let everybody that has done you wrong "Go". Holiness is letting go, even when I don't feel like it. It's not natural; it's an act of the will. Forgiveness is putting them on God's hook.

There is a difference between forgiveness and reconciliation. It takes two to reconcile (2 Corinthians 7) you open the door for Satan when you don't forgive. Unforgiveness allows bitterness to grow. (Ephesians 4:32) and grieves the Holy Ghost.

Check your heart. You need to have a good horizontal and a good vertical relationship. Some of the things that happen when you forgive are: It brings you to your purpose, you start being productive, and you increase patience. Forgiveness still ends you up in paradise. When you have forgiven you will ask God to forgive.

The psalmist said I've been there and my foot almost slipped (Psalms 27).

God will make every one of your enemies stumble and fall. He gives you a new table, a footstool, and a "Rock", the rock is Jesus. You say Father forgive them do not pick and choose. Forgive them all.

The Word says whosoever will let them come, who are they, your enemies not some but all, living or dead forgive them. Think about it, He forgave you.

Jesus died for all mankind He suffered the hurt for you. We are to do the same, forgive while it still hurts. No one needs to ask you to forgive, follow Christ, just do it.

## How to Endure the Cross
(St. Luke 23:33-43)

We hear the phrase "Hang on in there"

When times get hard, knowing how to do it, we have to have Jesus Christ showing us the way. It's not enough for us to watch Jesus hang there. We will have trouble. There will be times when we have to go there. There are some things that are just not permissible. God needs to get some glory out of your suffering. This represents God ordained and God allowed suffering. Are you aware of the cross of Christ Jesus and not aware of your own? Whatever your cross is God has orchestrated a glorified end. Some things that folks try on you won't work anymore. Take it from Jesus at the end of bearing your cross, it pays off. Christ never used anything at the cross supernatural. First lesson from the cross: When there is nothing that I can do what do I do? Often depression sets in on us when we get into a situation and there is nothing I can do to change it. Example money problems, you cannot make it come in. "But Jesus said Father" When you can't do anything else you can always pray. You say Father forgive them. You can never experience deliverance angry. It's a big thing to do when you are hanging and they are down there smiling. But you need to know and realize that you are going through what you are going through for the glory of God. In bearing and doing your cross you have got to ignore them. Because the one that speaks quick advice is not the one, be careful when a person has an ulterior motive. That thief on the left, I am glad that Jesus ignored him. The advice you get will affect everybody in your life. That's why (Psalms 1) says blessed is the man. When you go through don't lower your standards. You will give in to some stuff but I tell you "Hold On" don't second-guess yourself. My going through should not change who I am. If I say that I am healed, then I am healed. Because He is my help, my strength, and my all you should know whose you are. I belong to Christ Jesus. Knowing whose you are is going to pay off. Thank God for the man on the right, his words were let Him alone, be careful to stay compassionate. Sometimes you just don't feel like people. We would have possibly told him I am on the same cross that you are on. We have to give and break. Sit still; pray for others. We say what about me. Well, when you know whom you know and what you know on your lowest day you can still find strength. You are more powerful on the cross than you are on the ground. You never hear Jesus say these nails hurt. Don't get a hard heart because you are going through. Know that God will test (prove) you through others. Jesus died early to show others they did not take his life. "The cross only lasted but for a moment" The Lord Jesus went back to the Father. Be assured you may touch my body but you cannot touch my spirit. Therefore I know that no weapon that is formed against me shall prosper. Continue to look to Jesus the Author and Finisher of your faith.

# The God of the Valley

(1 Kings 20:28)

Favor in a famine

Elijah (the man of God) who is your Elijah? Glad you asked he is the one who prays for your soul. Your Pastor is your Elijah.

Ever watched someone go down because of bad attachments?

Ahab ended up bad because of who he was connected too, Jezebel.

We need to always attach ourselves with someone who has already been with the Lord. You are not the first one to go through and have a stronghold.

Ask yourself can God fix it? Yes He can. In (verse 10) Ben-Hadad said in (verse 12) the Lord said don't believe the enemy. In (verse 22) the prophet came back and said "Go" it won't end on this side.

The holier you get the bigger the war gets. In peacetime don't sleep, strengthen yourself, when trouble comes you don't have to pray long; when the storm comes you will be able to stand. Then you will be able to say I am here because I had the Lord before the storm broke out. (Verse 23) the devil gets mad at you when you win. While you are rejoicing he is plotting on you.

Right now no weapon formed against you shall prosper. They won because they were on a hill.

The enemy knew that the victory came from a supernatural force. It was a Deity that bought them through. They handcuffed him to the hill he woke up one of the prophets. He spoke the Word of God. He told Ahab he's coming.

God said today I will show them I AM the God of the valley. Praise God the same Word will bring you victory. That same Word is no new Word.

He sent them down to the valley. A whole lot of believers have handcuffed God to the hills.

When your dilemma has you depressed look to Jesus, when there is no way out look to Jesus.

Trust him with all of your heart to see you through for He is all you will ever need. He is our God of the valley.

## It Is Finished

(St. John 19:30)

Paid in full

What an Awesome statement said by our Lord and Savior Jesus Christ.

"It Is Finished" this is statement number six before Jesus gives up the ghost and goes back home to His Father in heaven.

It Is Finished lets us know that something has ended, and is complete.

In this case it is the sin debt that Jesus paid for all mankind. (It's all over the debt has been satisfied). When Jesus does something, figure out what the principles of it are. The affection statement, He says woman behold thy son, this is no giving up kind of statement.

You need to be able to look at some areas of your life and say when it is finished. Crucifixion death was known to last for days but Jesus brings His suffering to an end long before His enemies planned.

Don't stay on the cross past your time; you must declare that it is finished, let Satan know that he is a lie and that you will not follow him or be persuaded by him, (get yourself a radical praise). Jesus has already paid for your sin in full.

This was prophesying Jesus knew where He was going and what was about to happen. What they thought was hurting Him was getting Him to glory. You have to learn how to shout from the cups of pain. Do you know what your vinegar sponge is?

If so thank God for that vinegar sponge that has prompted you to know that it is moving time. The next thing scripture had already told is how he would act and look.

The scripture says I am blessed when people lie on me and I continue to do what the Word of God tells me to do. The Word of God assures me that joy is coming in the morning. Now fulfill what has been declared about you.

When we go through our "side effects" should not be as long lasting, all because of Jesus. When they came to the cross to break the bones they skipped Jesus and went to the other two. Don't worry about the piercing; the debt that we would have normally had to pay has been paid in full. Jesus paid it all! Now we must be good living sacrifices because he became sin for us. Some of those things that you are struggling with Jesus declared them finished. What a tragedy it would be for you to keep carrying around your sins.

Let the enemy know that it is finished. Speak it loud so that you can hear yourself, You need to learn how to tell yourself I am through with it, when Satan keeps trying to get you to do something hearing yourself will make the difference, it is finished, do you believe it?

# Over Coming The Obedience Obstacle

(St. Luke 5:1-11)

The key to it all

Obedience is the key to unlock divine blessings and favor.

Obedience is subjecting yourself to the will of another (voluntarily).

The Bible speaks a lot about obedience (Deuteronomy 11:27) (Acts 5:29) (John 15:5). You can't claim to love me if you are not obeying me.

You can fool people but you cannot fool God.

Obedience shows your level of favor; example "Jesus challenged Peter" He says to Peter lunge out into the deep.

Peter did it and caught many fish

Peter fished all night and caught nothing.

He was washing his nets, because he had failed.

When he obeyed Jesus things changed for the better.

Jesus will meet you where you are failing.

He is a Savior who sees something when there is nothing there.

What Christ is asking is not matching my life (my history).

Every man and woman in the Bible had to overcome.

Abraham obeyed Sarah, and Paul obeyed Jesus.

Obedience is better than sacrifice, "You cannot get what you want until you do what God wants you to do".

Folks who are not talking to God are weak in their obedience.

Don't pray, want obey, hitting and missing church.

You need to be there to get the Word; "some Word you will only get from your Pastor". (Hebrews 10:24-25) He toiled, and he worked, you don't obey God merely for your desire you obey God because of who He is.

Nevertheless, I can't see it but if you say so, obedience is not about a feeling, you need to take a trip to obedience before you get to faith, (Hebrews 11:6).

What do I do if I am just not there; your obedience has to be based on the Word of God obedience is the embryo of faith, it's the first step to getting there.

Obedience is the delivery room to faith! (So just do it).

Tap into it, like Peter did, he really got caught up with Jesus.

Obedience transforms into faith.

I have a fish from someone else's obedience; somebody prayed for me, the purpose of obedience is to have a relationship with my Lord. Some of us disobey when there is success, success alone will make you sink; try sowing into someone else's life you will be glad you did.

# How To Get Over It
(2 kings 5)

Let God take you there

Sometime you may want to tell people to get over it, but at some point somebody is going to have to tell me how. God cannot take you if you do not agree to go.

Things may be rough for you right now but you can get over it "no matter what it is". This verse is short but power packed.

In (verse 1) he was great because of his position he was somebody.

He was a leader, he was praised, everybody liked him, his performance was good, and he was great at what he did.

But Naaman was a leper; he was highly skilled at what he did.

But, just one bad weakness can make you forget about all of the good stuff in your life.

There are people on the outside looking in, and nobody has died.

The one that's living is driving you crazy; but your help is in the Lord.

Pray that God will help you to deal with that one weakness, that one stronghold that is keeping you from praising Him.

That one thing that keeps you isolated, if God does not fix it, it won't be fixed.

Naaman was the only leper at that time that was healed of leprosy.

Check out the young maid she was a good evangelist; she told his wife to go to the preacher. She was a person of faith, (St. Luke 4).

You have to know and understand that God can do anything but fail, so you need to be careful of what you are saying about the preacher.

His life depended on what she said, (the maid) he was trying to find help from the wrong king. If your king is not Jehovah kick him out! Okay.

You also need to know that sometimes friends can't help, Elijah said send him to me.

You want deliverance you have got to press your way.

Word was, tell him go wash, sometime you have to clean the outside before the inside gets better.

He gave him what he needed, we have to get rid of pride; and I thought.

Presumption- we have in mind how we want God to help us. God will not give you what you expect, but He will give you what you need.

He did not plan on participating in helping himself.

Many of us want our quick fix at the church; but it's what you do when you go out that is important to the Lord. God is not going to zap what you are going through.

You need to watch who you are with when you leave the church, because going home the wrong way could be the death of you. If you are going to be helped do what He says.

When it finally kicked in he was persistent he dipped himself in the river seven times.

Fix your mind, if I am going to do it, I am going to do it all by myself.

That takes a whole lot of faith; keep on doing what He tells you to do.

After all you are reading this now because I heard and I obeyed; to God be the glory, Amen.

# Getting To The Hem

(Matthew 9:20-22)

We have all got issues

We have issues that come and go some move in; some won't leave you alone.

The woman in this story had predominant issues.

How do you handle the one that won't leave you alone?

You can't talk about it at church you have it and are ashamed of it.

You are dealing with some things you dare not tell.

She had to make a right connection with the right person; and Jesus was passing by.

We become so ashamed to the point we won't even tell Jesus.

We struggle, and deal with the same things over and over again.

Instead of getting better you are getting worse. You have got to be willing to follow and touch the hem of His garment.

What made you get up?

What do you have to lose?

Why haven't you given up?

Because somewhere in there, there must be a hope (Psalms 27:13-14).

I would have fainted lest I believed.

God is going to turn it around for you, trust Him.

*Scattered Thoughts*

She was known sometime by her condition.

Sometime all people can see is your issue.

They come in dry and leave out dry; they are not trying to help you or themselves.

The woman figured something out, out of all the people in the crowd she knew she needed Jesus so she pressed her way.

It was not business as usual for her; she was ready to be delivered from her illness.

She did not say a word she just moved right along. God honors what is in your heart?

Because He knows that which is in your heart will soon get into your mouth.

She kept her will to be helped solely by Him.

What it is now and what it is going to be is two different things.

Nobody told her Jesus was in town she said it to herself.

Learning how to minister to yourself is a high calling of God, You need to say that no weapon that is formed against me shall prosper, and believe it. She had faith and proceeded to touch the hem of His garment.

She believed that the Lord had so much power that if she could just get close enough to touch Him, then all of her problems would be over. What do you believe?

Try Him and Trust Him, He will never fail you, He is Almighty God.

# Out Of The Box Praise

(St. Mark 14:3; St. John 12:3)

We must show signs of life

God wants us to have life about ourselves and be full of Joy.

He does not just want us saved from our sins.

Post-resurrection life you should have, and your praise ought to reflect it.

There is an ingredient required for everyone who has been redeemed from the hands of the enemy.

Your praise should tell on you, you should be identified by it, "Let everything that hath breath praise the Lord".

It's not about me when I think about the Lord and how good He is; I must praise His holy name.

When I think about His goodness compared to my dirty ways I can't help but to praise the name of Jesus.

When I think about the fact that I do not deserve to be here I can't help but to praise His name.

You don't deserve it either; this should make you want to change positions sometime.

If you could have only seen how my life looked before Jesus showed up.

That is why I am so grateful to Him; He loved me so that He gave me an opportunity to get it together.

That is enough for me to give Him praise daily.

Grateful to God is what you should be also; I challenge you to do something different today, (worship Him for who He is).

No matter where you find Mary she was praising God.

You have got to have an external kind of praise (it is the Alabaster Box Praise).

Hallelujah, I praise God for what He is about to do.

My break through is coming, my healing is coming, praise Him, and see what is coming for you?

Whatever it is, give Him the praise right now.

No one knows the cost of your praise, but you.

My praise does not fit in a box what about yours?

Now Praise Him, for He truly is Worthy.

# Set Up for A Miracle

(1 Kings 17:4-17)

God loves us so much

God will set you up!

You would not worry if you believed this.

God sometimes has strange ways of getting us to our miracle.

Be faithful and watch because God could be setting you up even now.

The sacrifice was a problem; look like He would have found somebody with a little more.

God really didn't need the woman in the story to get the job done.

God had already supplied Elijah with food twice a day by means of the raven at the Brook of Cherith.

How awesome, God can make a mean raven drop off groceries.

God changed the raven; God also knew that the woman needed Him in order to survive. (Psalms 24) the earth is the Lord's and the fullness thereof; it all belongs to Him.

He was looking after her needs, (Chapter 19).

He can get stuff done without you, you are not all that.

But know that He loves us more than we love ourselves and He includes us in whatever He chooses.

God's principles are eternal and they are true.

*Scattered Thoughts*

He sent Elijah to the woman's house because of what she needed.

When God asks you to give don't get mad because He is trying to help you.

You cannot make God richer no matter what you give because He owns it all.

Where do you start, when you need a miracle?

Good question, just use what you have; He will give you what you do not have.

God does not do supernatural first you have to do yours first, "I must be obedient".

God requires that I be a willing example "the man sick for thirty-eight years".

God said rise up and walk; and He obeyed and became a whole man.

If you obey God He will give you overflow.

God used the opportunity to pump the woman out of her comfort zone.

He does the same with us because He loves us so very much.

God bless those who are already doing something in your name.

Let God tell you what He wants you to do.

Give Him all that you have, and then in return He will pour back into you. To God is the glory, Amen

# I'm Still Here

(Daniel 6:7-10; 16-23)

When you become powerless it is then that you recognize how powerful God is

Kneeling represents humbleness. You can pray anywhere any time and no one will ever know it, but you and God.

First I am impressed with God in this lesson. Second I am impressed with Daniel. In his first demonic plot Darius wanted to be above Daniel.

But they could not find anything on Daniel "in verse three we find that Daniel had an excellent spirit in him".

When people come at you they will go through a group of folk just to get to you. They will do whatever they can to bring you down.

We need to be like Daniel the only thing they could find was that Daniel was a godly man.

In verses seven through nine they set out to ruin him. The devil wants to ruin you also be warned that he will do whatever he can to take you out and to destroy you.

It does not matter if it is as an individual or as a family, he is coming.

Daniel didn't just serve God, he reverences Him; those that were around him did all they could to trap him, but while they were plotting, Daniel was praying.

We need to do the same, simply because of what may come our way.

If you stay prayed up you will be in a position to give it over to Jesus, and let Him handle it, all because vengeance belongs to the Lord.

A lot of us get angry or what have you, and we want to handle things ourselves, but when we do, all we do is mess it up.

If you let the Lord handle it He will bring you forth as gold.

Daniel did not wait on the problem he prayed it out, his prayer was a prayer of thanksgiving, and this was a comforting prayer.

Jerusalem represented their hope in an eternal God; it was their symbol "the Jews". Daniel was very sincere in his prayer, but he still ended up in the lion's den. What is your lion's den? A situation may look bad, but, there's always hope, trust God in everything.

# A Sin In A Mercy Situation

(1 Chronicles1: 7-8; 13)

On Jordan's stormy banks I stand

David said I sin greatly for I have done this thing.

Let me fall into the hands of the Lord and not into the hands of man.

What if there was no soul satisfaction, children of God would suffer.

The church must take a stand and tell the world that God has a solution for the sinfulness of our day.

The Psalmist tells us that His mercy endures forever.

Thank you God for mercy and grace, all of us at some point in life have acted foolishly. But thanks are to God, for He has forgiven us and blessed us beyond belief.

Therefore, we should always keep a humble spirit that God might use us in His service. We were made for the Father, made in His image and likeness (Genesis 1:26).

Our God has no use for do nothing people, He wants us to wear out not rust out, so if you are not busy, get busy for Him.

If you are idle, then you are a sitting duck for the devil and his angels, he has nothing to do but go to and fro in the earth looking to destroy the lives of men, women, boys, and girls.

He never gets tired because he wants as much company in hell as he can possibly have, don't be fooled, and don't be a victim.

If you have given him your hand snatch it away, come back to the Father, he is waiting on you, and He will forgive you of all your sins.

Choose you this day that you will serve.

My prayer is that you will choose "The Lord God". For He is waiting on you, to walk with you, wants you to join him today.

# Dealing With The Devil

(St. Luke 4:2)

Anything short of His perfect will is a sin

Every time Jesus had a confrontation with the devil not at any time did He resort to His supernatural power?

Jesus is all Sovereign in the flesh so he can do anything He wants to at any time, however he wants to.

Jesus deals with Satan as a man so that we would know how to deal with him in this world.

I praise God that He deals with Satan so that I don't have to take anything from him. (St. Luke 4:1) in order to handle Satan you have to be full of "The Spirit".

You cannot handle him by yourself, you cannot out smart him.

Satan knows what it is that you like better than you do.

We have to become more like the Spirit-led Jesus Christ.

Jesus did not play his games, and we certainly should not play with him either.

The only way to defeat the devil is to put your trust in Jesus, and let the Holy Ghost help you as you walk, He will direct you all the way.

In every area of your life you must trust Jesus.

The devil will offer you things he can't give you; he will get you out there on that limb by yourself and go on to the next weak person.

You must be full of the Word, full of "The Spirit", and fully committed; in order to make it in your Christian walk, let

Jesus lead you all the way, this way you will be sure not to fail.

## Dealing With The Devil Round Two

(Numbers 13:31-33)

Be not weary in well doing.

Satan now is even angrier but I now have a remedy the Word of God. (St. Luke 4:13) Know that Satan did come back to Jesus.

Our Lord was Awesome, and He never talked about dying without talking about getting up. Jesus said He was going to get up. Satan is always making rounds.

God had promised them the promised land, I believe the Lord, I believe He died for me, I believe that one day He is coming back for me, I believe that He has prepared a place in heaven just for me, what do you believe?

You either believe the Lord or you believe the devil. Who is ruling you? The Lord is ruling you or you are being ruled by the devil, only you know.

How do you know? You know by the life that you lead, and you know by whom you obey. If you have stopped acknowledging God then you are definitely on the side of the devil, doing what he wants you to do.

You need to get with the Lord and let Him bless you; if you go for it by yourself you will mess up every time.

Let the Lord bless you according to His holy will. You see when our blessings come before time they can hurt us.

You need to pray and make sure that it is God who is calling you into the blessing. Talk to Him He is waiting on you.

They based their success on their own strength. Who are you basing yours on?

I can do nothing of my own power but (Ephesians 4:13) tells me I can do all things through Christ who gives me the strength.

They started talking about what they were able to do, you need to recognize that you can't do it, but realize that it can be done.

Your extremities are God's opportunities; this could have easily been their strongest point or their weakest point (v.31).

What about you? Be aware of the enemy at all times, he is certainly aware of you.

Know that you have the victory, and that your victory is in Jesus Christ our Lord.

He won the battle for you on the cross at Calvary, "Praise Him now"!

## The Bush That Burns

(Exodus 3:2-5)

We all need the Bush experience

We can learn from the bush and apply it to our Christian life. Every person who has given his or her life to Christ needs to have a bush encounter. It can help us in our individual life as well as our Christian life. We must realize that as children of God there comes a time when we must make a change, there comes a time when we cannot remain where we are, we cannot remain the same.

Becoming a child of God puts a demand on our lives. I am no longer under my own control to do with myself as I please I belong to Him.

As children of God we have been bought with a price, Jesus Christ died for us; and for our sins, that is how much the Lord God loved you and me.

Moses is our great example in these Scriptures; he could have walked away from the bush yet he did not.

He chose to approach the bush he chose to obey the voice of Almighty God.

When God calls you listen and obey. Because call you He will.

God trained Moses in the second stage of his life at the burning bush.

There comes a time in life when I need to catch on fire (Spiritually) in the name of Jesus Christ.

There are too many fires burning externally and not enough fires burning internally. There is only one way to ignite the fire.

It is the Word of God. You must study His Word in order to grow. There are too many dry bushes in the house of God and the reason is lack of knowledge.

The Word is there but you refuse to receive it. The Word is in your home but you refuse to read it.

What bush are you? Whose bush are you? Make sure that you are tapped into the right source. "Jesus Christ" then your flame will never go out. Hallelujah, Amen.

## Did You Forget To Say Thanks?
(St. Luke 17:11-19)

He's just too good to forget

It is a dangerous thing when Christians go from day to day and don't say thank you to their Father.

They simply said Lord have mercy on us. Because of mercy the world was given a chance. Mercy is who Jesus is.

Everybody wants rights but don't go to God with that, because if you got what you really deserved you would be dead and so would I.

It is God's mercy that is keeping us. Every man born into the world came with the disease called sin.

The only way to be cured from leprosy was by divine intervention because there was no cure for it, and there is no cure for sin.

Yet all of those with the disease were healed, but only the one came back.

The reason is that he recognized who Jesus was and returned to give the Lord the glory and honor that He deserved He glorified God. We should do the same because He is to be honored and adored by those who He created, called, and chose.

Let everything that has breath praise the Lord.

How many times do we have unrecognized blessings? He's keeping you in good health; you are not suffering for lack of food, clothing, shelter, or a place to lay your weary head. Most of us have more than enough. May the Lord continue to have mercy, even at this present moment in

## Scattered Thoughts

our lives; I cannot even begin to count the endless times He has blessed me, my family, friends, and on and on.

You really don't know right now at this very moment how blessed you are.

Jesus is saying to us even now remember my good teaching and be well mannered.

Thank you Lord, it is because of you that we are blessed.

# Do Not Play With God

(St. Luke 1:20)

It's very dangerous to disbelieve

It is a dangerous thing to hear and reject the Word of God, or merely just don't recognize Him for who He truly is. He is to be adored, honored, worshiped, and praised.

This was no ordinary man this was Zechariah who had prayed for a son, and his wife. Yet he did not believe God. You can see in this verse God is not pleased. No one ever wants to talk about God's other side but He does have one.

We need to pray that we stay right in His sight; we need to pray to be better people, we need to pray that we not violate this temple that we have given back to Him to use as He pleases.

We need to live holy not just on Sunday but every day of our Christian lives. (Romans 12:1) we need to be steadfast (1 Corinthians 15:58) we need to apply the Word in every area of our lives (Proverbs 19:24) God is very disappointed with us when we do not apply the Word to our lives.

The Lord has been too good to us for us to live just any kind of way. We are to be examples to those around us. Those who have not caught on yet to this blessing that we share. We are not to walk like the sinner because the Grace of God has saved us.

It is past time for us to show the world how to live. There are people out there that need to be saved; there are people out there that need to know that we are serious about our Father in heaven.

Let's be real, and be that light, which we know we can and should be; because somebody needs you, and they need to see the Jesus in you. What are you going to do about it? It's moving time, in the name of Jesus. I truly do believe God.

# God's Word Benefits Us

(St. Luke 1:38)

I am used for His glory

Every time I hear the Word of God it ought to have an impact on me! It is not so much what I hear but what I do when I hear it.

God's Word requires action on my part. God's Word gives us benefit, when He speaks His Word begins to work.

His Word is the living Word. In the beginning was the Word and the Word was God the Word became flesh and lives with us (Jesus Christ) "The living Word".

The Word caused Mary to see herself. It should and will do the same for you but you must open yourself up to Him.

The angel was Gabriel the "Arch angel" We should always, as children of God, be open to His call.

After all it is not about you or me it is about Kingdom building.

Those of us who are saved are pregnant with great opportunities to do His holy will. When God finds favor with you that is in itself a great honor.

We have to stay in the Word (The Bible) then the Word will get into you (God the Holy Ghost).

Don't give into the things of this world, be led by the Spirit of God. It is past the time of being lazy; we must be about our Father's business.

Jesus Christ loved us so much that He died for us. The least we can do is serve Him.

We should work and not complain, wherever he has placed you be satisfied, because there is a reason for you being where you are. It's time to deliver. To God is the glory, Amen.

# The Power Is In The Command
(John 5:8)

We have the ability to do

Sometimes God will bless you based on your condition. Sometimes he blesses us just because He is God.

Jesus asks the man who had been on his bed of affliction for thirty-eight years do you want to be made whole? His excuse was I have no man. What's yours?

Then the Lord told him rise up, take up thy bed and walk.

He speaks to us the same way, your blessing is right in front of you, but you are to crippled to go and get it. Get up take up your bed and walk!

You have been in this predicament to long; can't you see the hand of Jesus reaching out to you. All you have to do is reach out.

The blessing is divine don't you want it? Reach. Aren't you tired of the enemy riding you and wearing you down each and every day of your life? Reach. Can't you feel the power of almighty God moving through you? Reach.

You have been enabled by Almighty God to do whatever it is that He would have you do, and to do it well.

Reach, The Lord God is not asking you to do anything that you cannot do. Reach. It is past the time of just looking at your condition or the state there of. Trust Jesus and reach. He is standing right there ready to heal you, help you, and pull you through.

God has given us the ability to do! Jesus does not give blank or empty commands.

Hear me, when I tell you, the power is in the command, reach. Rise up and walk.

# You Can Make It

(Jeremiah 29:11)

"I AM" has planned it

This is enough to give me joy to know that God has planned my life before the beginning of time, whatever you are destined to be God planned it.

We get side tracked in our young years and Lord have mercy some of us even in our old ones. We get deceived by our own self-will, and by the enemy.

But there comes a time when we must wake up, and know; that there is really something wrong with this picture.

We have all been created with a built in sensor that lets us know that God is real.

Now that you know it is up to you as to what you are going to do with it, and how you will apply it.

 If you are not where you are supposed to be, now is the time to get there. I am so glad that He is patient; and is teaching us how to be patient in His Word.

God gives us ample time to get it together. But He is also "Our Father" He gets tired of our mess.

Well guess what its breakthrough time. We have all had storms in our lives and felt as though God did not care, but He does.

His Word tells us to cast all of our cares on Him, because He cares for us. There are going to be days when the sun is going to shine in your life, and there are going to be days when there will be cloud burst.

But God is right there, some of these storms He allows just to get you to your place of destination.

When God is in your midst, there will always be "Son" shine, because Jesus is the light of the world.

Faith can hold you in the storm; and you will come out victorious if you trust Him.

Seek and you shall find, knock, and the door will be opened, it's your time.

# The Gospel Says You Can Be Saved

(Romans 5:19)

Truth is I may be a sinner

Sin leads to the death of the spirit, the affections of one man affected so many for so long. We are all living with the same blood that flowed through Adam.

Therefore you will sin, and do whatever pleases you; you will not respect your fellow man, nor do you respect yourself.

You do not worry about who is watching you, or for that matter, imitating you.

Sin grows like a cancer; as long as this blood flows through you and you never move to make a change, you will be a sinner until you die.

Sadly so, you are already lost and at the end, and you will be lost forever, in this state of mind. But, there is hope. His name is Jesus. He died for all mankind.

Your life can only change when you come into the knowledge that you do need someone greater than yourself. It is then and only then, when your change will come.

Does this sound familiar to you? If so today is your day. Give yourself to Jesus.

The Last Adam made us Free (Jesus Christ). The first Adam brought death.

You must be born again from the flesh to the spirit. (Romans 10:9) gives us the steps to becoming saved 1. Accept Jesus as your Lord and Savior 2. Believe that He died on the cross for your sins and that He rose 3. Confess that you are a sinner who needs saving. 4. Ask the Lord Jesus to come into your heart as your Lord and savior, right now. If you followed these steps you are saved, let someone know of your Salvation, get into a church that is teaching and preaching the Word of God. Where you can be baptized, grow spiritually, and live according to His holy will. (1 John 4:4) tells us that greater is He that is in me (Jesus Christ) than he that is in the world (the enemy the devil). Congratulations you are now a child of the King.

# When You Feel Like Giving Up

(Psalms 27:13-14)

What is keeping you?

It is easy to show God in your life when things are going good. But when things are not going as well do we praise Him?

The world is full of its ups and downs, highs and lows; and this is not going well, I don't know what to do scenarios.

We have an adversary who is doing all that he can to bring us down to destroy us. And if we are not careful he is going to succeed with some of us.

We must learn to put our trust in the Lord. No matter how bad things may get, or seem He will bring you through.

Don't give up! Don't lose hope! Yes we have all been down and depressed at some point in our lives. It can, and will happen even to the best of us.

Some think that they are indispensable, well you are not. As a matter of fact you are the ones that will soon fall. So, never rely on you.

You can fall at any time without the Lord. So stay wrapped up in Jesus and His holy Word. Let the Holy Spirit have complete control of your life. You will be glad that you did.

David is our example in this scripture, without Jesus, you will certainly faint.

Let Him be your "Great Emancipator", Heart Regulator, Burden Bearer, and Heavy Load Sharer. Who else but

Jesus can carry your load? The answer, no one. He is our all and all, Hallelujah, Amen.

## His Will Be Done

(Matthew 6:10)

Are you doing the Lord's will or just going through the motions?

Is my work according to the will of the Lord or am I just doing something to be doing something.

Is it for man to pat me on the back and say oh my, or is it all about Him?

Are you a leader over a Ministry? How do you act when serving? Do you exemplify Christ like qualities or are you doing your own thing?

How do you make others feel when they are around you? Do they see the Jesus in you or do they just see you?

Well my brothers and sisters if the answer to any of these questions is yes you have a lot of work to do.

Number one you need to repent, ask God to forgive you for getting in His way. Then let the Holy Ghost take control.

As children of God we are merely servants that should, and must; yield our will to Him. After all, He has been too good to us, Jesus Christ died for us.

So for us to be mean and indifferent to others and say we know Jesus is not going to cut it.

I thank God that He is no respecter of persons; we are all equal in His eyes. Everyone who gives their life back to Christ is His child, He loves them and they are precious in His sight.

Therefore they should be precious to you too. It does not matter the years or the minutes they have been a Christian, they have a place in His house; they have been gifted and should be placed where they will be of the most value.

If His will is to be accomplished in the earth (you) we have to get in sync with the Holy Ghost who is our leader and guide.

Then we can say, and truly mean what we pray, when we pray, Thy will be done in me. Amen.

## Jesus Wisdom

(St. John 2:12-25)

Jesus knows what is in you

Jesus knows what is inside of all of us. He does not need us to tell him anything, or to help Him for that matter.

He is God the Son! He knows all things. He knows your intentions, whether they are good or bad.

He knows your thoughts. He knows when you will give; He knows when you do not give. He knows when you are sincere, and when you are not.

He knows when you are doing things just to get what you want.

We must as Christians, learn to live as Christ lived and walked. It is most important that we do things according to His will or we will find ourselves in the same predicament as those in today's Scripture; Getting thrown out of the temple because of their self will. You must realize that The Lord knows your heart, He made you; nothing gets by Him. There is a saying that is very true "you can fool man some of the time but at no time can you fool God". Therefore you are only fooling yourself and being made a fool of.

Being obedient to His Word is most important. If you are really born again that will be of utmost importance to you also.

He is our role model, if you needed one I say to you today look past man and look to Jesus. He is the one who died for your sins; He is the one who delivered you out of the hands of the enemy (Satan) we should be most grateful and appreciative today for His saving grace.

Breathe this prayer of thanksgiving to the Lord today; simply saying Oh Lord God; I am so thankful that you love me and care for me, even when I am not loveable and into myself, you stand with open arms, waiting to forgive me, over and over, now Lord, I pray your forgiveness, help me, to put first things first; especially you, in the name of Jesus I pray, Amen.

## Good Things Bad Boy

(St. Luke 15:11-24)

This could be you or me for that matter

Many things grab our attention and cause us to go after the things of this world.

You cannot and should not continue to let the green grass fool you. There in the grass are snakes and thorns waiting to trip you up and draw you away from the Lord. You need to know that everything you need, God's got it.

There is good in each of us. You should give your every care to Jesus.

His Word tells us that He is our burden bearer.

There is an element of good in each of us, example the coin. You just have to get into the right hands.

The boy just wanted what belonged to him he did not ask for anything more. We should be very thankful for what we have and not begrudge others for what they have been blessed with.

Another thing about this young man was that he did not say and do any and everything in his father's house.

He came out; some of us want to do what we want to do, regardless of where we are.

If you don't respect yourself, you are certainly not going to respect anyone else, nor their house.

Let God change you, let Him lead you and guide you, because when you have depleted all of your sources of income, etc. He will be there waiting with open arms ready and willing to take you back, praise you Lord for your goodness.

# When Jesus Is Inside

(St. Luke 1:39-42)

Let Him In

What cause these events to take place? When Mary was with Elisabeth it had to be that Jesus was inside.

When we are saved the Holy Ghost seals us.

You could not look at Mary and tell that she was pregnant, but Jesus was down inside. When Jesus is living inside of you, you will go, we say come, but Jesus says go. Mary went to help Elisabeth.

When Jesus lives inside of you, you will not keep it to yourself. You are filled with the Holy Ghost and if Jesus is inside it will stir up others, even sinners. Getting others to Christ requires that you know Jesus.

Things happen when Jesus is inside. Jesus keeps us from having the spirit of jealousy. Elisabeth could have been but she was not, she accepted the blessing that God had given unto her womb.

She encouraged Mary, and she knew that truly Mary had been chosen to carry the Savior of the world.

She honored her and celebrated with her, she shared in her joy.

As a Christian you must have the spirit of discernment so that you know exactly who to follow.

You must learn how to hold on to your joy and continue to trust and depend on Jesus. Continue to give the Lord the praise, the honor, and the glory that He so deserves.

Mary spent time in the Word; that is why she could say His mercy.

Now you should be able to say as Mary said, Lord, do with me as you please.

Stay in the Word of God because He wants and desires to have a personal relationship with you; are you willing to let God have His way in your life?

# What Made Them Wise Men?

(St. Matthew 2:1)

Look for Jesus

In the secular world they were wise men. Education does not make you wise nor does age, this is a true statement. Yet there are Christians who think like this!

Jesus was at least six months old when they arrived. They believed for every special man there was a special star.

They were educated but had no spiritual insight. We say they had educated sense but no common sense.

Sometime we can be too smart for our own good. What makes me wise? I am wise when I desire to see Jesus.

They wanted to see Jesus. They followed His star. If you are going to get to Jesus you must follow Him in His Word.

They were exceeding glad with joy, before they even saw Him. What is your level of joy when it comes to seeking Jesus? You must be careful where you stop. Sometime we stop short of just where we need to be.

Sometime we get right to the door and turn around; when you seek Him, you need to keep on coming. He is waiting on you.

Let your life be a testimony for someone else. You are the pattern that someone else is watching, when you witness bring the message clear where they can understand and follow.

When you come to Jesus in His Word He never fails to give us instruction as to what we are to do or where we are to go.

These men had no problem giving, they opened their treasures up to Him and they gave to the Lord good gifts.

When you follow the Lord He will take care of you. Because of their faithfulness God warned them and they left and went back another way.

Don't go back the same way you came because there may be trouble on that road.

Get right instruction then you will know the way that you are to go.

# Blessings Are Plenty

(Matthew 5:1-11)

Reason's to rejoice

Some of us are in places we should not be! God has decided to allow us to be where we are in order to teach us and mold us.

Some people act like they made it and did things on their own.

But He promises for the believer a life of blessings.

For those who are obedient, sometimes we put a comma; when God puts a period. (Leviticus 10:10) God demands that there be a strict difference between believer's and the world.

We must put a difference between holy and un-holy, clean and un-clean (Deuteronomy 28) curses.

God wants obedience from his children, obedience makes the difference it say's who's I am.

God makes you what He wants to make you.

If God wants you to pastor, pastor, teach, teach, encourage, encourage, give you know, give.

Christ was good just for the sake of doing so. Not only was He good, He was meek, He was not a bully.

We need to be very careful of how we mix with people, what is your reason for doing what you do, what is your ulterior motive?

Let everything you do be about the business of the Kingdom of Almighty God.

If I am to rejoice this is how it will be done. God should always be first and foremost in our lives. After all it is not about you or me.

I rejoice in the fact that He has given me an opportunity to be an instrument of His holy will. I know that a day is coming when I will receive my just reward.

A reward that is far greater than anything that man could ever award me with. The glory belongs to God, Amen. Rejoice and be exceeding glad (v.12) for you are not alone.

# What Did Jesus See?

(St. Mark 12:41-44)

Jesus is looking

We like for Him to watch. We sing the song angels keep watching over me. We quote the scripture He never slumbers nor sleeps. We talk about how He watches over our children. We sing the song His eye is on the sparrow and I know He watches over me. We sing the song let the light from your lighthouse shine on me.

 We ask the Lord to watch over the church, our pastor, choir, family, home, etc. We ask the Lord to watch over everything but our money.

 Jesus last trip, before He went to the cross, He took a seat where He could check out all these folks who claimed to love Him so much. He saw how they gave.

People don't like you watching when they give. The Kingdom of God does not grow just from singing and music. But it grows from the giving. The love of money will always cause problems. For instance: Cain and Abel, the rich young ruler, and Judas.

Judas sold Jesus for thirty pieces of silver. In the book of Acts two people were killed because of their lies about the money they had and were able to give.

The church in Acts almost fell out because of money. You even get angry because of people messing over your money. I know that's right.

As Jesus sat in the temple and watched the people give He called His disciples and said come look at this poor widow woman.

He gives her accolades as giving more than the others.

You won't give your last if you don't trust whom you serve. When you've got heart, you have got a cheerful heart. The Word tells us that where your heart is, there your treasure will be also.

So stop letting "I Love You" walk around naked. Stop tipping God the way you do the restaurant when you eat out.

You are letting your attitude show when you know His Word but yet you choose to do it your way.

Learn how to tithe, that is your starting point. The offering is the beginning of the believer. You have not done anything until you learn how to give an offering beyond the tithe, because the tithe already belongs to God.

The widow woman gave her all. The others gave out of what they had left.

Don't try and brag on who gave the most because that is something that you do not know. God is blessing you right now, so give. Jesus shows how big my sacrifice is when I give.

## The Life
(St. John 11:25)

Jesus wants you to do all that you can

You have to have a now faith and keep it before you. Jesus said "I AM", never will you find Him in the past tense. You need to know that God is here right now. "I AM the Superior.

He calls Himself the resurrection because that's who He is. He is the only resurrection that got up and didn't go back down. I bless Jesus for not having to die any more.

God wants you more than just saved; He wants you to have life. Don't just be saved and satisfied.

There is a certain attitude that a believer ought to have. It looks like we get saved and give up the life part of it.

Sinners have fun, Christians are mad all the time. Christians need to laugh (v.35) Here Jesus wept He was not crying about Lazarus dying. Jesus came to raise him up. When you know what the Lord has said to you, you don't have to cry over it.

There is a level of pain that I would not have if it wasn't for trials.

Trouble will teach you how to shout. Its one thing to be messed up when you don't have Jesus, but to have Him and still be messed up, Lord have mercy.

Some people may think you are strange because you get knocked down and are able to get right back up, sometimes things can happen in life that really throws us off; but I come to tell you that Satan really is a lie.

*Scattered Thoughts*

Our mood swings and attitudes are a reflection of our belief, real belief altars how I act; if you believe God can hold you in your mid-night hours it will show up in what you do. Jesus is saying to us, who have placed stones to cover our hurt; you can put away the stones "I AM" here.

Jesus did not move the stones for the mourning women, He says you can do that yourself; Jesus wants you to do all that you can, (He told Moses at the river go forward) He needs you this day and every day, to go as far as you can go.

## How To Recover

(1 Kings 19:1-4)

Are you tired of fighting?

I am! Well, God gives us another chance the same as He did Elijah, He revives Elijah again.

The same thing it takes to have spiritual burn out it takes to recover.

Yes we all have spiritual lows, because there is a condition on the inside of man.

There is a void; a spiritual low will exhaust you.

Now is the time that you must fix your mind and know that Satan is not going to leave you alone.

Therefore you must have the right mindset, you see Satan left Jesus alone for a season, so why would you think that he is not going to keep coming at you?

The Word tells us to resist the devil and he will flee from you, but could that be the problem? That many Christians are not really resisting.

We need to have the mindset that Jesus is not going to leave us alone either, Thank God. If you are going to get over your spiritual burnout it depends on the kind of bread you are going to eat. The raven bought the divine bread to Elijah in small portions, the bread that you should be receiving now, as a Christian is the Word of God.

With this bread you certainly do not have to worry about getting too full. You do not have to worry about getting heartburn or indigestion. You do not have to worry about your mind over working, or trying to solve problems that are not yours to solve.

How do you get up from your spiritual high? You need to trust God to do for you what He did for Elijah at the brook and what He did for the widow. He did it all because of her obedience to the preacher, she had more than she would ever need, she lived and so did her son, and even after he died he was brought back to life by Elijah.

Don't click when things are not going the way you think that they should, because God knows what is best for us all.

She made the cake of bread from the handful of flour that she had left, and gave it to Elijah first, and then she and her son did eat. Doing it God's way is the way. Has God spoken to you through your pastor? Were you obedient? Get connected to a spiritual person, so that you can grow according to God's holy will. You are no longer your own boss; you have been bought with a price.

# I Made It Through The Night

(Daniel 6:7-10; 16-23)

Night is coming!

It rains on the just as well as the unjust, and you need to know that night is coming to you, how soon? Only Jesus knows its preparation time, look at Daniel; he kneeled upon his knees and prayed three times a day, and gave thanks to God. How is your prayer life? Daniel saw the storm coming and still had time to pray.

It is important that we pray for ourselves and not wait and depend on others to do it for us.

Some people depend on the pastor, friends, or the members of the church to pray for them.

Sometime we are put in situations where only we can pray, there is no time allowed for calling in others. This is how the Lord God wants it; we are to depend upon Him.

Our nation is in trouble because of lack of prayer, our homes, schools, churches, and friends are to.

Prayer is essential in the life of a believer, Daniel was in trouble all by himself; but he never stops trusting God. Have you ever been there? Yes, we all have.

When you are alone; or just feeling alone, that is the time to call upon the name of the Lord.

The first thing here is the devils plot against him. (Verse seven). Satan has a brand new problem to present today that has been tailor made to fit only you. Question is what are you going to do with it? Will you try and solve it, or will you give it to Jesus? Only you know the answer.

Daniel prayed while they were plotting, his prayer was not a crisis prayer.

He prayed a prayer of confidence; that is what we must learn to do.

When you are going through you must know what to pray for according to what you have to deal with at that particular time. And the only way that you are going to know is to get into the "Word of God and let the Word of God get into you". There is no situation that God cannot handle, let Him have it, and watch Him work. Yes, He can; and will turn your night into day, if you will only let Him.

## Not Bowing Down
(Daniel 3:17)

Who are you bowing too?

Have you ever found yourself in trouble for doing the right thing? Well standing up for right will get you in trouble more than anything else.

But these men were able to see beyond the problem to their solution; people did not influence them.

Nations went down and worshipped, but they did not participate, you have to be very careful of what you involve yourself in, because it may be very detrimental to your wellbeing, to your very soul. You need to stand, even if you have to stand by yourself; and stand by yourself sometimes you will.

It is not a comfortable place at first, but when you realize that Jesus is there with you it just gets easier each time.

Don't be persuaded by your friends, because they will certainly try to influence you to their way.

When you let go of something; keep on going, don't give in to the pressures of this world. There is a day coming when you will be rewarded for holding on, stand, no matter what or whom it involves; because there is no one greater than the Lord Jesus Christ.

A lot of us are surrounded daily by the ungodly and we fall to what they are saying and doing.

Do not let these kind of people cause you to make bad choices as well as be influenced by them.

They are not being led by the Word of God, so you have to continue doing what is right, because right, is just the right thing to do.

You are the one who will have to give an account of how you acted and what you did in your body, not those whom you chose to follow, and listened to.

We need to be just like the Hebrew boys and say I will not bow down, because I know without a shadow of a doubt that our God will deliver us, and, if not; I will still be better off than you. Please do continue to "STAND", in the name of Jesus Christ our Lord, Amen.

## Saul's Damascus Road Experience

(Acts 9:3- 6)

He will get your attention one way or another!

Let's take a look at Saul's resume, he was multi-talented (Philippians 3) he was a Hebrew; he was on the Sanhedrin Council and over the Pharisees and Sadducees. Amazingly Paul went to church he just did not know Jesus.

That is why there was a need of the Damascus road experience. Some are in church now and still need to have a Damascus road experience, because just coming and going through the motions is not enough.

Make sure when you enter the sanctuary that you meet the Father, and share with Him; let Him take you to where He wants you to go.

Give Him the honor and praise that He so deserves. One thing that is missing in the life of most Christians is that they are simply not letting the Holy Spirit rule and reign in their lives.

There is no way around salvation. You must give your life totally over to The Lord. There is no proof of Saul doing the killing, but he certainly had a hand in it. He voted to cast the stone.

When the Lord came upon Saul on the road he fell to the earth (verse four) he humbled himself.

No one can stand in the presence of Almighty God. It's a good thing to humble you, (verse five). Saul asks the question who art thou Lord (recognition). Sadly so, but some of us do not know who Jesus really is!

*Scattered Thoughts*

When you don't know who He is; it will affect your actions, Saul never saw Jesus in the flesh, but He was told by the Lord what he was doing; Christ said, what you are doing you are doing to me. The Lord God takes it personal when His children are hurt.

Saul's question to Jesus was what do you want me to do? He did not make a request; this lets us know that we need to hear the Lord, and what He is saying to us.

He is saying to most Christians today, stop walking out of your calling.

You are in a hurry to do, and have not been anointed to do, wait on Jesus.

The answer comes in (verse six), get up and go; when the Lord speaks that is the time to rise up, rise above, and go to your calling as a conqueror, and more than a conqueror. Saul could not see, he had to be led to his destination; when he got to the right place and to the right person his eyes were opened. The same way he was led you have to be led. You cannot, and should not, go out in any kind of way in the name of Jesus. And when you lead, make sure that you lead people to the right house. God has saved and filled you up with the Spirit. Saul was on his way to raise hell, but he ended up being the preacher of the hour. He ended up on a street called straight, if you are tired of living any and every kind of way; then today is your day to move on to the street called straight, you see, there is a place for you.

# What Gate Are You At?

(Acts 3:2)

Are you coming or are you going?

This man kept coming and going home, there are many gates: gates of religion, gates of understanding, gates of being delivered, gates of cussing, gates of fussing, gates of shacking, gates of drinking, and gates of mad and angry. There are many others gates, and I am sure you have even come up with a few on your own.

Most of us are flowing through the gates of come mad and leave mad, never satisfied about anything.

What is keeping you at the gate that you are standing in front of? Some Christians have been at the gate for so long, that they just don't want to go any further.

There comes a time in your Christian walk when you should want to move past your gate, and the only way you are going to do this is by having a heart change, way deep down on the inside; and no one can do this without the help of "The Holy Ghost".

I am amazed at the fact that some come to the house of God and change, and others come and go, and remain the same.

How is it that over time some people grow up; and others continues to fail?

This man was born lame, and so were we, born with some kind of shortcoming.

This is the part I just love, but thanks be to God He changed it, we were all born a part of the Adams family, in other words it's in our blood (sin).

He was carried every day (the man) well some of us are carried to, and it is way too much. As children of God, there comes a time that you must learn to stand on your own; but, only with the help of the Holy Ghost.

Being carried does not help; it just makes the situation worse. He was faithful to what he believed. Somebody should have said man look, stop taking the long way to hell.

We all need help at one time or another in our life situations. But the only satisfaction that we will ever receive will be from within.

Jesus Christ made the difference for us by going on the Cross-at Calvary, He died for our sins. Therefore we who have accepted Him have received our blood transfusion; which has changed us from the inside out. He is what makes the difference in our lives, Jesus Christ, the second Adam. The glory belongs to God.

# Loving My Enemies

(St. Matthew 5:43-44)

How to do it

We are to love and do well by everyone even our enemies. Our lives must line up with what we say we believe.

I believe the Word of God, what about you? I have been through a lot in my life with people, but there is one thing that I have learned to do without shadow of doubt, and that is to give all of my troubles over to the Lord.

We say we love the Lord, but cannot get along with one another, oh my! I know that I am on it.

One of our soul purposes should be to share with each other, are you sharing? I have come to let you know that it is wake up time.

No one person is any better than the other, even though some people really believe that they are; well I am going to give you the opportunity here to get over yourself, and this is how you will do it. According to the Word of God, you are saved, so you are a new creature. It's time for you to let the old man go, with those old ways that are not yours.

When we start to live like God wants us to live, and then things begin to happen for us, good things.

He will find favor with you, and begins to use you as it pleases Him.

Now that you have been made aware of the fact that you are a new person, beware; because you are now on Satan's hit list.

Paul and Agrippa loved in spite of: But we will say precious Lord Take my hand, and have a problem shaking hands. (Galatians 6:10) tells us to do good to all men. Hebrews tells us to let brotherly love continue; get rid of those ill feelings.

Example: I didn't think of it first so I am angry or as we love to say mad.

She thinks she is better than me, so I am mad, and it goes on and on.

I know you can think of one yourself or maybe even more than one.

Jesus Christ was addressing all men who were to follow after Him, we must stay prayed up. Because Jesus loves us, He, has not asked us to do anything that He Himself has not already done.

He is our greatest example, and I need no other, this is what makes it so much easier for me, try it, because it really does work.

# What Prayer Does For Me

(St. Luke 22:31-32)

Wait on God

When you go into prayer wait on God to speak to you; He will do the rest. Prayer is not a fast food service, even though we tend to treat it as such.

Another thing that we do is that we will wait until we are worn out, and then give the Lord our worse.

Praying every way but the way that we have been directed to pray, the Lord gives us the ability to fix things ourselves. He will not vanish all of our problems; some of them He leaves for us to go through and deal with. That is the only way that we will grow as Christians.

He gives us the power to handle our own problems, but do we handle them, or try and pass them on to someone else?

That is why we need to pray, because prayer helps us to overcome, and it helps us too grow out of our comfort zones. It also puts us on a path of change to trusting and believing, in the Lord God. I know that I can, because I am His.

Prayer transforms us (2 Corinthians 2:12) into what we are called to be. (Romans 8:28) All things work together for the good to them that love the Lord who are called according to His purpose, (not ours but His).

When you get burden, don't let your burdens get you down; praise God, hold your head up high, and walk in the name of Jesus according to His holy will.

Even when you are not feeling it, do it anyway, it works it is life changing. (Jesus said in verse 42) if it is your will let this cup pass. Well we know the Word and the Word tells us it was not in the will of the Father to do so, and the cup was not moved.

That lets us know that there are some things that we must endure; there are some cups you must turn up and drink from.

Praise God today for your cup. My cup released me into great and better things, but it did not happen until I turned it up and drank.

# Are You Teachable?

(Psalms 25:4-5)

Only you have the answer

As Christians we should be teachable, no one man knows everything. In order to be teachable you must be reachable, if you have an attitude of nobody can tell me anything then you have a grave problem.

The Lord spoke these words before He was crucified, (He said "I AM" going but there is one coming who would lead us into all truth; Jesus called Him the Spirit of Truth).

He was speaking of the Holy Ghost who is now present in the lives of all that are saved. He is the one who gets no recognition, but He should. We always like to go past Him who is in us, (Holy Ghost). He is all we will ever need in this world.

But we choose to call our friends, and love ones, for help when help is ever present. Does that make any sense? Glad you ask because you already know the answer.

But in case you don't the answer is no, we refuse to hear Him, yet He speaks to us each and every day.

When will you start hearing what He is saying to you? There are a lot of things we have gotten ourselves into, we have a lot of debt that could have been avoided, a lot of a lot of, and they are all because we chose to do things our way;

As a matter of fact most Christians are still doing and living the way they choose. My statement to you is, that you should be tired of the same scenario every day, every month, every year, let Him have it.

When the Lord changes us we are changed for the better, and I feel that you realize by now, that your way really does not work. Don't you think by now that it is about time for you to try the right way?

David petitions the Lord to show him His ways, and teach him His paths. The only way you are going to walk right and be guided right is by the Holy Ghost.

This is Divine knowledge that only comes from God no mere man can give this to you. David further stated that God is the God of His salvation, He continues to ask to be taught and led into the truth; and then He states I am waiting on you all day, no matter how long it takes, wait on Him, because He certainly does know what is best for your life, so let your steps be ordered by the Lord, now read, meditate, and pray.

# Is God Ever Too Late?

(Mark 5:22-23; 35)

He slows down on purpose

I must go to God in prayer in every situation and circumstance in my life, and I must also realize that prayer does not move me from my problem.

As a matter of fact sometimes it will hold me right there, God does this for the purpose of growing us up in Him. He wants me to grow in my problems because all of our trials come to make us strong.

He is teaching us how to endure hardships, no matter what the hardship may be; when I endure my hardship I will come through, as gold, and I will prosper.

We sometimes in our lives try to make God move by our actions, we cry, have tantrums, and other things, but God is not impressed with that at all. He moves in His own good time, because He can see what we cannot see, and He knows what is best for us.

In these verses Jairus goes to Jesus in a hurry, we need to approach the throne of grace humbly; because nothing is due us.

If we got what we truly deserved we would have been on our way to hell, But God loves us so much He gave us His darling Son Jesus Christ.

Jairus fell at the feet of Jesus expressing the sickness of his little girl, and asking for help, wouldn't we all? Falling at the feet of Jesus, show that he is humble, even though he is troubled. He also came hoping, some of us pray out of ritual, not out of hope; you must believe what you pray or your prayer will not be answered.

When he came it was in haste, and he went directly to the source, The Lord Jesus, you need to realize that you are powerful because you are a child of the Most High King. He has given you the ability to deal with any and all situations. You should also be aware of the fact that sometimes before a thing gets better it may get worse, so was the case with Jairus daughter.

While he was talking to Jesus he was informed that his daughter had died, it cannot get any worse than that, But Jesus spoke as soon as He heard the word and said don't be afraid only believe. To believe Him is to trust Him, because of his belief his daughter was raised from her sleep (verse 38). To us that which seems dead is only asleep in the eyes of the master. If you have something or someone that needs to be revived let the Lord do the raising, expect it to come to pass, believe it in your heart, and then receive the blessing that He has for you.

# She Came Crooked But She Left Straight

(St. Luke 13:11-13)

What about you?

We cannot look down on this woman who needed to be healed of her sickness, Why not? Because many of us are exact copies of what she represents, she had become content being in this state of crookedness.

We too tend to be most comfortable in the state that we are in, we hear the Word of God but we just cannot see ourselves changing. We can see everybody else's fault but we think within ourselves, oh I am all right. Well I want you to know that you are deceiving yourself.

You need to see within yourself that there is a need to change, because number one God cannot, and will not use you in your state of crookedness. Every time you hear the Word God, He is saying; my child it is time for you to straighten up, and He means right now. One thing that I can say about this woman is, that regardless of her state, she made it to church (verse 11).

This lets me know that she was not comfortable where she was, when you are sick, or going through, the house of God is the place where you should be. His Word is what you need; you should come in running because that is where your help is.

Don't let the enemy (Satan) keep robbing you of your blessings, instead have that in spite of attitude and watch God move in your life. Who was teaching in the temple? Jesus.

My Lord and my God here is your healing, in the Name of Jesus straighten up.

Be assured that you cannot do this on your own; this is why God put the "Under Shepherd" in the house "The Pastor, Teacher, Preacher".

Get in a good house where the Word of God is going forth, and you will begin to grow straight, and into where He is calling you. Be assured now, Jesus is calling you. Sometimes we cannot see it, because of the crooked state that we are in.

When you are crooked over you are always looking down, Jesus could be right in front of you and you would not know it. She was in her crooked state for eighteen years. How long have you been in yours? Today is your day to be delivered, He can and will lift you up. Jesus called her to Him even before she could see Him, (verse 12) watch out now.

His words to her were "Woman" thou art loosed, those are healing words from the Lord Himself, Hallelujah, Amen.

She was freed, and you can be also, but what you have to realize is that your problem is not on the outside it is on the inside. (Verse16) Satan will make you sick. But Jesus knows that our problems are not just physical, that is why He heals us, there is a place on the inside of you that belongs to Him, and until you let Him in, you will remain in a crooked state, won't you let Him in today and be made whole.

## Can You Say Yes Again?

(1 Kings 17:10-16)

What do you really mean when you say yes?

Yes Lord, yes to His Lordship, yes to discipleship, the more chances He gives me the more I ought to say yes to Him, to His will, to His way. No matter where I am God wants me to say yes.

Our Christian life should be a continuous yes. God took care of Elijah at the Brook. It will be the same for you when you get your desires to line up with the promises of God. Then He will give freely to you.

The Psalmist tells us that we are to delight ourselves in the Lord and He will give us the desires of our heart.

 Elijah found the widow woman-gathering sticks, where will God find you?

You should have already said yes to salvation, yes to sanctification, yes to dedication, if not, God needs your yes today.

God will challenge your commitment to Him, the first yes was free.

Ever ask yourself what and whom are you committed to? The second yes came with a price; it was the sacrifice of Jesus Christ life for our sins. God wants that yes that will cause you to move out of your comfort zone, (Romans 12:1).

 So stop asking for what you want, and do what He tells you to do, I know that most Christians don't want to do this because it is going to cause you to lose something that you want to hold on to, that something is called control.

Get rid of that me, my, and I syndrome; and get into the He, and His.

Let God know that you are totally His because you have been born again, and that changed everything.

So whose orders are you going to follow, His or yours? Be totally His, which is the only way, He is teaching us how to trust Him (Verse 12), and her focus was messed up.

How can I say God lives in me; until I redirect my focus, and I do that by faith. Faith teaches us, it shows us how to face our fears (Psalm 27).

If you are fearful, faith is not in the house; and it will be missing. Trusting teaches us how to respond in faith. The woman responded in faith, faith shows up in how you walk.

The second yes teaches us and directs us to our destiny. Know that we are all here for the purpose of doing something, (verse 9). It is up to you to find out what your purpose is. And when it is revealed to you, remember; who it is that you serve and live for daily, and obey Him, because, it is definitely; not about you.

## Job's Shoes
(Job 1:1)

Can you stand wearing them?

If you chose to listen to the advice of everybody who gave it to you, you would be naked, broke, single, unemployed, busted, and disgusted, just to name a few. How do you think you would do if you were to walk in Job's shoes? It's very easy to talk a subject when everything is going well in your life, but what about when the war is raging in your life. (Verses 6-8) Let me tell you this, it is no accident when you go through a Job experience.

God has put you in those shoes; or either He is allowing you to be in them, and if He has allowed it to come to you, it is because He knows that He can depend on you to handle it.

No matter what we go through we must love God for who He is, (The All Sovereign God).

Now you go ahead and go through for Him, because someone needs to know that you are in the Lord; and that there is a higher calling on your life.

After all this is your witness for Him, so that man may know and see that God is real in you

When you belong to God He can use us however He wishes. The Word of God tells us that He will put no more on us than we can bear, and the truth is that He will not.

But I know for a fact that at times it seems just the opposite. When you follow the will of God you make the devil shame.

How am I to respond in my situations? (Verses 20-21) says blessed be the Name of the Lord; right here is where most Christians are falling short.

Not blessing His name the way that He desires it to be blessed, it's not a do it when I want to do it, it is an everyday all day thing.

The Psalmist says: I will bless the Lord at all times and His praise shall continually be in my mouth, that's Word, Job said, though He slays me yet will I trust in Him.

No matter how long He allows you to stay in it "Trust Him" and continue to worship Him.

Everything that the Lord allows us to go through has a beginning date, a go through period of time, and last but not least an ending date. Just think about it, somewhere along life's way you have been through something; but, in the end, He delivered you.

So praise Him when you go in, and praise Him coming out. There is a reality to everything that man has to go through, Job recognized that, and tells us that a man born of a woman is of a few days; and those few days are full of trouble (Job 14:1). Therefore you should not be shocked at what comes at you, because you are always going to have some kind of problems.

Just endure them for your deliverance is coming, all you have to do is reach out, and hold on to God's unchanging hand, and then; you can say like Job, I shall come forth as gold, (Job 23:10), in other words; it is God who purifies us, and then you will know for certain that you are better because of it (Job 42:12), so we thank you now God for our trials.

# God Will Provide

(Genesis 22:1-14)

I know that's right

God will prove you, so don't you think that you are fooling Him not for even one second; there comes a time when He will put you to the test. (Verse1) God did it, and when He does call you into testing; you should be able to trust Him and endure.

There is confidence in just knowing Him, and that helps when you get into pressurized situations that you certainly cannot handle.

Being confident will help you to keep your nerves calm, and your belief in God will help you to go through.

We worry needlessly, but being able to look into the life of Abraham, can and will help us, because he is teaching all Christians a very valuable lesson.

Lesson number one, we must know that God is still as able now, as He was back then; to do whatever you need Him to do.

There are some things we cannot change, we allow the things of life to worry us and control us, things we have no power over, such as sickness, running to the doctor, bills, etc.

Abraham was seventy-five years old before he even began to work, and God waited twenty-five more years before He blessed him with a son.

In everything that God does there is a purpose, His first source of testing and many of our problems are within us. So who are you going to blame? We cannot blame anybody but our own selves.

Some of the things that come to us are through Satan, but when you have the Lord God; He will get him out. God gives us the strength and power to overcome and to do what we need to do to get Satan out of our lives.

When you are tested it is not to lead you into sin, God does it to see how loyal and faithful you will be to Him.

You see a true believer will keep going, no matter what; when there is no money, when there is sickness, and when they are not receiving the blessings they want. Now, ask yourself this question, do you love God because He is God, or is it because of the job he gave you, or that husband, or that wife, or that house, or those children, etc? Good question.

What is your Isaac? If God took it away would you still love Him and serve Him?

I must remind you here that Job lost everything, but he still trusted God (Job 14:1). Abraham needed to pass the test because someone else was waiting on the results, (you and I are that someone else), and he did not doubt, Abraham said, we are going, but, we will be back, this is unshakable faith. Your blessing comes to pull you closer to God; not to drive you away.

## Do It God's Way

(Exodus 3:10-11; 14.)

His way is the way

What is the problem with us doing things God's way? Well to be truthful, the number one problem is self.

We are no different from Moses in our lesson scripture today, the first thing that I want to do is tell God, about my I can't, okay; God does not want to hear that.

He already knows what you are capable of, after all it was God who created you and called you to Him.

Don't you think that He is intelligent enough to give you what you need in order to fulfill your purpose in life!

He knows your abilities and your disabilities, just like Moses some of us are still in spiritual bondage, why on earth is that?

Because I just cannot believe that God wants to and can use me in His service.

The only reason God is not using you is that you have not yielded your will too Him, it is way past that time, you need to let go and let God.

How is it that; as a Christian, I can trust everything and everyone but God? Something to think about, does this fit you? If so it is re-dressing time, He has giving you a new man, let him rule.

He gave you the Holy Ghost, let Him have His way, and watch your life change for the better praise God and put your trust in Him. Can you trust Him today? Or will you continue like the children of Israel choosing to stay in bondage, over giving in to a Mighty God like ours.

Don't have the Israelite syndrome, because forty days turned into forty years, my Lord. Let's be like the bush and catch on fire instead, the bush was saying something, and it caught the attention of everything and everyone that was around it.

Everything that goes on in the church should be because of the voice of the Lord God Almighty.

You need to crucify self; and do it God's way, because He certainly knows what is best for you, and for His house, it is time to go to work, children of the most High God. Now be thankful for your growth stage; and trust His timing to release you to His work, Amen.

# Battling For My Blessing

(St. John 5:4)

He blesses at the right time

I praise God that He knows exactly where I am, I don't have to worry about someone else receiving what my Father has for me, I never think that maybe He has forgotten my address or anything like that, because He knows where I am at all times, He's God. Sometime we need to be encouraged, because a lot of Christians tend to think that maybe God has forgotten them, especially when they are going through; especially when sitting back and watching blessings flow to others, you may wonder "Lord, how long", I have been in this holding pattern for a long time, and I see no breakthrough in sight.

Just like the man waiting on someone to help him into the water, what was he battling against? How long had he been sick? Time was against him, but time also makes us think.

We say God is late, that's denial. Time makes us do some crazy things, and think some crazy thoughts, ever thought or maybe even said to someone it seems as though my name is broke.

Sometimes our condition causes us to give up, and it is much more severe when it is the condition and not the circumstance, for example you may have trouble on the job; husband or wife issues, money funny or not at all, children just as nutty as they can be, etc. That is merely your circumstances, the verse tells us that Jesus knows. Aren't you glad He knows? You should feel better just because of the fact that He knows.

You have to go to him for yourself; because man does not care about you, you ask, "The Lord" for what you want, and believe that it is done, and He shall bring it to pass.

I can truly say that my blessings fit me just the way that they are supposed to; you need to watch that crowd.

The People believed that an angel came and stirred the water (v. 7), and according to local tradition the first one in the water would be healed, but, the Bible nowhere teaches this kind of superstition, this would have been a most cruel contest for many ill people, "Our God", does not work like that. Aren't you glad? He is a merciful God.

———————————

# Men and Women Trying To Do It Their Way

(Genesis 16:1-6)

It won't work

I am sure you will agree at the onset of this reading that all we do is make things worse when we try and fix them.

God knows, that we need to get out of His way, and let Him have His way, in our lives; God knows that He has to work on us; to get us ready for many of our blessings.

Our problem is that we don't want to wait on Him.

That is why a lot of Christians are so messed up, choosing your own job's, even when finding that special someone, or as we say my soul mate, and I know that's right.

Some of the biggest messes that we get in, we do it on our own, warning, warning; it is a dangerous thing to venture out on your own, and do it your way.

We don't like to bring up the ugly points about a good person, yet they are there, the Word of God tells us that all have sinned and fall short of the glory of God, "key word, all".

 God likes to get us to that point where we know for a fact we can't do whatever it is that we are trying to do.

In Abraham's case he was eighty-five years old and still no son, he became very frustrated.

Dealing with the man, God is holding him responsible, you must be held accountable for your actions, yes, all of us.

A man will give up everything for sex; he did it because he wanted a son. (Man of God why are you doing it?) It got Abraham in trouble, what do you think it is going to lead to with you? It does not take but a minute to get you in trouble.

Dealing with Women, Sari as she was called then had it all planned out; we never think about the repercussions of what we set up, and come up with, okay.

Women are very vindictive and naïve, jealous of one another, and afraid of being out done.

We readily want to take positions that do not belong to us, so don't come down on her (Sari) see yourself in this lesson, be honest with yourself, and by being honest with yourself, God can, and will, make you better.

Men of God get in your rightful places, and lead.

Woman of God get in yours and let him lead the way. This will only work if we do it God's way, (Proverbs 3:5-6) states, Lean not...let God direct your path, read it and grow.

## They Stood Together
(Daniel 3:16)

Let's stand please

We find these men in a lot of trouble, as a matter of fact, you could call it death row, Daniel had been prompted to Babylon, and he said that he was going to carry everyone he could with him.

Daniel made sure that the Hebrew boy's had positions; you know it is all right for a person to be jealous, but when they become envious you have a problem.

That says they want to be where you are, crazy as it may sound it is the truth.

They don't know what you went through to get there, all they know is they want it.

I pray that if you are ever faced with a situation or challenged in anyway concerning your love for the Lord; that you will be able to stand, even if it requires you to stand alone; and believe me sometimes it will require just that.

The Hebrew boys made a covenant and that covenant was to stand; no matter what the outcome, even unto death, what about you? They stood for righteousness, they stood for what they believed and in whom they believed, and they also stood together.

Know where in the Word of God, will you find, where one was mentioned without the other.

They are the most awesomely bonded together group of believers I have ever read about, or ever encountered anywhere; that shows us that it is good to have a faithful few who believe, and become unified in their beliefs, than to have a great number that is just making a lot of noise and saying nothing.

It is not pleasing to God, and most of the time, it is not doing anything for man either, we have to be real, because real is who we were created to be.

How can I help those that are lost, if I am lost too? We need to consider the consequences just as they did, they trusted what God would do, (verse 17), they were convinced of His capabilities; and they had concrete conviction.

The great crowd went down; the island of three stood up, and somebody noticed.

They were three men, with one God (Jehovah), when it looks like the odds are against you, trust the Lord God. He is for you, and He is more than this world against you, what an awesome combination, the Lord Jesus Christ and us.

# What Made Him So Blessed

(Psalm 1:1-3)

You can be also

Do you measure blessings by what you have? What I have is not my blessing, some people have a lot but they are not blessed. Some have a little, but they are truly happy now that's blessed.

My blessings come from within, he was separated from wickedness, and he did not stand in the midst of bad activities.

You need to know just as he knew where you are to sit. Christians should always know where they are to sit.

It's not a good thing to be a Christian and always get caught up in all the wrong places. You should know who to run with, and who not to run with, because somebody is watching you.

You are to be an example, not join in with the rest of the world, keep yourself in the Word of God, and you will be okay.

If you are being talked about it's really okay, because they talked about Jesus.

Jesus is the best and greatest example man ever had, or will have because He is still alive. You don't have to do those ugly things that come to your mind, you have the Holy Ghost, and He is just waiting for you to let Him have His way, (You do know that an idol mind is the devil's workshop? If not I am making you aware of it right now.

Omission leads to Commission: a man, who does not recognize God, is a dangerous man. You must sanctify your environment, don't be hindered by others, don't speak ill of one another, and keep yourself separated from bad attitudes, because what you say can and does affect others.

God is trying to take you higher, you need to keep your mind on Him, and not take the advice of the ungodly.

All advice is not good advice, it may sound like it, but it is not.

To be truly blessed you must separate yourself, and saturate yourself with your inner man, then hear the Word of the Lord, you see a blessed man is one who hears, does, and lives the Word of God.

What you take in, is exactly what you are going to come out with, he was also blessed because he situated himself by the river of living waters.

 He was planted in the right place; not just planted, and no man gets the credit for that only God, Hallelujah, Amen.

## How To Overcome Fear

(Isaiah 41:10)

Help I'm terrified

There is no need whatsoever to fear, when you have the Lord God Almighty. There is not a better person to be on your side, He is always watching over you.

Trust Him to lead you all the way, we worry about things we have no control over, and our mind is constantly on everything but the Lord.

How am I going to pay the bills? The checking account is overdrawn.

Does it not seem to be a little bit much, to keep carrying on like this? Knowing there is really nothing you can do to make it right, why not put your trust in Him, (Jesus). Believe God, and pray, and, believe God.

You must learn how to overcome fear, before fear overtakes you, fear is something that works from the inside out, it is a mind thing, and it comes at the Christian more than any other evil I can think of.

We are really fearful of the things that we anticipate, but you can be delivered from all of this by trusting and believing God, when He is present there is no fear.

When we fear there is no faith, fear causes us to act un-rational and lose control, we even go as far as to say I am scared, when we talk like this we are not trusting God, and when we speak like that we disappoint Him.

Because we are saying that God cannot handle our little mediocre problems, some things are for us to go through that is a part of our growth stage.

God made a promise to us, and placed His holy angels around us, to watch over us, and that is why we have made it thus far.

We are recognized by the provisions of God because He is "I AM" *my favorite*.

The next thing you need to realize is that you have power over the enemy; God has not given us the spirit of fear, but of power, love, and a sound mind, (2 Timothy 1:7).

Faith and fear cannot live in the same house (you), now call forth your faith that kicks out your fear, and tell the devil that you have your help, His name is Jesus, say it boldly, and say with Authority. To God is the glory.

*Scattered Thoughts*

# How To Deal With Pain

(John 11:32)

Calling 911 wont do

I can really relate to this one, this is not a stay away from subject because this is something most Christians deal with on a day-to-day basis.

There are all kinds of illnesses that cause pain, and there are other issues, which cause pain also, it does not have to be a sickness.

You know the real truth is that most people don't want anyone to know their area of suffering. What to do:

First realize that we do not have to fight any battle of our own accord, yet many are doing just that.

There is someone who is so close to you, and He is just waiting on you to give out, and give in, His name for those of you who have been away for a while is Jesus, and He can and will heal you.

One thing we need to remember is that it may not be His will at this particular time to do so, sometimes we have to go through in order to be a help to others, somewhere down this road of life.

There is one more thing that you need to know, if you have a physical illness, be aware of the fact that all sickness is not unto death.

Now this is what you need to do; I call it help yourself time, get into the Word of God and let Him speak to you, Pray daily, meditate on His Word, find where in the Bible the Scriptures are that line up with what you are going through, and let them begin to minister to you, healing is in His Word.

When was the last time you talked to your heavenly Father? We have a strange way of showing our affection to someone we call our friend.

Yet we want Him to come and do this and do that, we call Jesus our friend and want and want from Him.

My question to you is what have you done for Him lately? Mary is a good reflection of many of us who say Jesus is my friend. Some of us are good at hiding what hurts us, let me give you an example; Smiling on the outside, yet dying on the inside from something that has really hurt you, it is time to face your pain, because pain that is not given the attention it should be given does not go away.

All it does is gets more intense, some pain gets so out of control that it causes depression, and for some the loss of their life, (sad but true).

The main thing pain wants to do is, get your attention off of whom it needs to be on; He is the Lord. No matter how bad you think the situation is, you do not need to take your eyes off of Jesus, healing is in His name, if your pain makes you cry; call Jesus, if the doctors gave you a bad report call Jesus, if you have a spouse or children that are causing you pain call Jesus, I could go on and on, but I feel you have the big picture. If you are ready to be delivered, show the Lord where the pain is, because it is His desire that you be well and prosper.

# How To Treat Jesus

(John12: 1-3)

"HE IS MY I AM"

What does the Lord really mean to you?

Is He just a name running around in your head?

Does He have significance in your life?

Well only you my Brother and Sisters can put answers to these questions.

Do you ever miss saying thank you for all of the blessings you receive?

This is "The Man" who has and is still doing everything that He can and ever will be done for you.

Jesus never complained He just did what He came to do.

Now it is up to you and me, to go forth in His name, doing what He has commissioned us to do.

It should not be hard to serve someone who gave His all for you; you should not even have to think about it.

When He speaks, your response should be, yes Lord, whatever you want me to do.

Where does He really stand in your life today?

Is your work more important than the work of your Lord and Savior?

How's your worship?

Are you praising and blessing Him; or are all these things that I fore stated a dilemma for you?

If so, you have got to get it together, you cannot claim to be a Christian, and never move in the things that He has told you to do. You see God is waiting on you to honor, praise, and bless Him, after all that is what you were created to do; you are in debited to Him, He owes you nothing.

He is a loving and patient God.

But, He does get tired of our so-called agendas, taking His place. It's time to get our priorities in the correct order.

We need to be like Mary, Martha, and Lazarus; after all we do have a place in Him. Martha served, Mary sacrificed, Lazarus, sat at the table with Him, where's your place?

If you don't know get in a Bible believing church where you can learn and grow.

God will certainly show you, and when you come into His presence, come with a thankful and grateful heart; come, giving your all to Him, for He is so worthy.

It may just be your last chance; only God knows for sure, do all that you can while you still have the time, and if you love Him like you say, show Him, It makes Him happy, and it also pleases Him.

## Your Needs Are Always Met
(Philippians 4:19)

Yes He will

No matter how bad things get you should count it an honor to be chosen by God to live the life that you are now living, it is not by chance that you are here.

God loves you so much that He gave (Jesus). That was really the ultimate sacrifice,

So what am I doing?

Sitting around trying to figure out within myself the how's and the why's of life.

God is too good for me to even go there, but go there I have.

He is righteous, faithful, patient, long suffering; He is the light of this world, yet you just can't seem to get it.

I know without a shadow of a doubt that there has never been a time that He has not provided for me, as long as I can remember God has been blessing.

If you are ever going to know Him as your God, you must learn to trust Him.

God has put everything and everyone in the Hands of His darling Son, Jesus Christ that includes you!

Paul wrote this letter from the prison, and he still finds joy in writing it.

What he's saying is this; no matter how rough it may seem to have gotten, or how tough it gets, you should do the same, always count it all joy.

No matter what the situation, God still is and always will be God.

He wants your problems today because He is the problem solver; your part in this is to let Him have it, Whatever it is.

Then you must believe, that He can; and will do what no one else can for you, with you, and through you.

That's faith and trust; now that you know He is your source, rest in Him.

It makes a big difference when I move out of the way and allow God to be God.

It would be a good thing to keep this before you daily.

He will supply "ALL", not some; whatever you are lacking in or short of God's got it, Hallelujah, Amen.

# What Makes You Sing?

(Luke 1:46)

Is your heart glad?

Every believer ought to have a song; well, I certainly know that is true.

Throughout Scripture they always had a song to sing.

When the Israelites came out of Egypt they had a song, Paul and Silas sang so good in the prison that the cell doors came open; that was some kind of praise.

David had a song coming out of his grief in the loss of his son (some of us sing for the wrong reason), some sing because that is their gift.

Mary had a song in her heart, Mary sang because she had been in the presence of the Lord.

I should not have to wait until I am in corporate worship to sing, there are things that happen in our lives every day that should move us to sing unto the Lord.

If Jesus is ruling inside of you there is always going to be a song in your heart.

I don't have to hear anyone too want to sing.

It comes straight out of heaven, and flows down into my very soul.

Your life will tell on you, I realize that every song is not the kind that you would want to present to the Father, but Christians are getting down with them.

There are some songs that even the Christian ear should not entertain yet they do, that calls for change of lifestyle, "Oh yes, holiness is a life style".

You cannot live any and every kind of way through the week and then expect to bless God with your mess on Sunday.

Some of you are walking around looking crazy trying to figure out what's wrong, well now you know; you cannot change in and out of spirits like that, you are either for Him or against Him, so now, whose are you?

It is decision time, Mary was glad because she had been informed of her mission in this world.

It is going to be awfully hard to minister to someone when you yourself need to be ministered too.

Mary had the power of the Holy Ghost to come upon her (verse 35), you have the Holy Ghost within you, that's truly power and a big change, you have the power to change the world, but it will only happen by being obedient to the Word of God.

It's not about singing good; it's about singing with power, when you let the Holy Ghost rule, and reign you will sing with much power.

So trust Him now to make you most effective as you let go, and let God.

## There Is A Need
(Acts 2:2-6)

Revive Us Lord

What is your connection in the church, are you that spiritually strong person that she needs, or are you that weak link, either or, you could be helping or hurting the house of God?

The church needs strong Christian leaders and followers; are you a saved person, well certainly then, you are a child of God?

They were first called people of the way, now they are called His children, His people.

There are some "His people" who have some very wicked ways, and do some very wicked things, what amazes me is that they never give it a second thought, they just do it and keep going.

Kind of makes you wonder; also a little scary, when you really think about it, and yes, they confess daily to being a child of God.

We were all born into sin; Adam is the only man that was born into the image of God. We need to take a spiritual look at ourselves, and who better to do it than you, no I am for real, seriously, really look; I know that you do not like what you see, because we are never satisfied with what we have, we are always trying to outdo one another; and this thing has even infiltrated the church.

This it is just crazy; but it's okay though, because none of us were born the way God intended us to be, that is why we had to have a Savior, and be born again.

I am so glad that He loves us enough to give us a second chance, a chance to get it right, before we are called out of this world.

You do not have to die lame, just trust Jesus to bring you out, don't continue on this merry go round of I am just me; no you are not, you have the Holy Ghost living inside of you, and that makes you greatness; you are the Lord's to do with as He pleases. Once you accept your change don't go back, and don't be influenced by those around you; if you have to walk alone to make it, do it.

Be careful of where you allow yourself to go, and be careful of those you take with you, because everywhere you go, He is there.

Also be aware of the fact that others are watching you, and you will be held accountable for your actions, and know that the Lord Jesus sees all; and knows all, He is the "Soul" judge, so be revived, and be renewed in Him.

## What's Wrong Worshiper?

(Psalm 34:1-4)

It's about The Lord.

When you come into the house of God, worship should be done according, as it pleases Him, the Word of God says let everything that has breath praise the Lord, even a baby gives praise to the Lord, in the way He was created to do it, even the animals praise Him.

I have sit in my home and watched the trees, how they bow to Him in praise, and they don't breathe as we do, that's a fact we are to worship God simply because He's God, not for what I can get or for what I have received, praise Him, because He is God and He is worthy.

We should be like David, he said I will, David was committed to being consistent in his worship, and we should do the same, every Christian should have a time that they commit unto the Lord.

We are so busy doing our everyday stuff that we have forgotten Him who is really important, Jesus.

Oh yes, and about the breath thing; if it were not for Him, you would not be breathing, you would be out of here quick, fast, and in a hurry.

But because He loves us so much He is giving you every opportunity to get it together regardless of what is going on, we have to learn how to say, Hallelujah anyhow, and mean it.

A lot of Christians have that I am going to wait and see attitude, oh well, I was told growing up as a young girl many times that wait broke the bridge, didn't understand it then but I sure do now, and I know that you do too. If not guess what, Jesus is in the house, and you have missed him. You are to be ready to praise Him at all times, this is not something you have set up in your mind, He set it up in His Word a long time ago, and all you have to do is follow His Word.

You really don't have to be pumped and primed to praise Him; all you have to do is just do it.

God said that's enough, if you just stay in His Word, His Word will begin to live and move in you.

That's a fact, the Soul of a man that is saved and knows it, gets happy, in the presence of Almighty God, it's your time, to Praise the Lord.

## The Church

(Matthew 16:18)

We have been called out

We have turned the church into so many different things; things it was not meant to be, some have made it a hangout place, some a gathering spot, there has not yet been a head change, but a hangout change, some look at it as a place to court, dating and mating, and some are saying I have paid my dues, now I will do what I want to do, wrong answer; if you are a Christian you should do things according to the will of God.

And we all know that His will is Holy; and that it is right.

What does Christ really mean when He asks the question, "Whom do men say that "I" the Son of Man AM"? (Verse13). We must confess as Peter did; His answer was; thou art the Christ, The Son of the Living God, do you really know Him?

Jesus is not suggesting that He's building His church on Peter, what He is saying is "I AM" building on what Peter had said.

We have no stock in the church, because the church belongs to the Lord, and Christ is the cornerstone; He is the one who makes sure that everything works out right; therefore everything ought to point directly to Him.

One individual can make a Christian, but only Jesus Christ can make up the Church.

Jesus has already made a way for us to get back that which belongs to us, gates are used for two things; one is to keep something or someone in and the other is to keep something or someone out.

Who have you left at the gate? It is definitely recovery time, trust Jesus to go with you to the gate and recover that which belongs to you, it may be a family member, a friend, or it may even be you, whatever the case may be, go and do it now in the name of Jesus.

# A Salty Church

(Matthew 5:13)

There ought to be a standard.

Again I say to you everything about the church ought to center around Jesus, Matthew's gospel tells us what we ought to be, the people of the world are getting worse; our churches are bland not salty.

The text does not say you will be; or you ought to be, but it states that we are the salt of the earth.

The other analogy is you are the light of the world, we do know that "Salt purifies". Therefore, there ought to be a standard about us that demands people to act a certain way around us, salt keeps you from becoming rotten.

We preserve things around us every day, so what about your inner man, if you plan on being what God would have you to become you need to stay in His Word,

God has preserved my soul for Him alone, one day we will go home to be with the Lord,

It will not be this outer shell but the inner man.

You should be salty enough to help make the world a better place; we need to go to the Lord each and every day.

We are being fed daily through the study of His Word so that we can go out and feed the needs of others.

The best and quickest way to kill a church is by doing nothing; let me make something very clear to you dear friend, you are the church, and you must be fed.

It is not enough to give the Lord your life and continue to do the things that are pleasing to you.

It is time that you let the Holy Ghost rule, because He is present in you, He is laying dormant in some, and has so long until it is just unreal and also sad.

I pray, that today, you will have a change of heart, and let Holy Ghost have his way.

Are you adding anything to you, so that you can encourage, and help someone else? There is a great danger of not going back to the Lord who is your source for what you need.

Can your salt be tasted or is it so contaminated that all it is good for is to be thrown out? If you answered yes to this question its okay, just ask God to give you back your salt, and He will.

# First Love Forgotten

(Revelation 2:1-5)

The Church forgot

The Church at Ephesus was a major Church, and it was also a major city.

This was not the only letter, there were seven in all, and it shows us one or two things,

One is that all Churches are not alike; it shows us then and it shows us now that they were all addressed to the angel of the Church.

"The angel of the church for those who do not know is the Pastor".

If you are not, or do not have a church home, you need to get in a good one, let the Holy Ghost lead you in your search, find one that is a Bible teaching, and Bible believing church.

The letters also describe Jesus and lets us know that He can be whatever we need, or want Him to be; He also gives a promise of reward to the person, the individual.

He promises if you overcome He will reward you for your diligent service.

There were great concerns in this church. God has placed the church here to teach and give the Word.

They were a busy church, so busy that Jesus said; I know your labor.

When we labor, we sweat; when we study, we carry out a work; when we work, that is something that we choose to do, such as holding a position, etc.

Things don't just happen we are to make them happen.

This church would not tolerate evil in their midst.

It is past the time that we should be about the business of the Father, (God).

When you work you're busy, but when you labor, you get the job done.

So be encouraged in the fact that Jesus is still the one in charge; that is truly more than enough to keep you going.

# Let God Be God

(1 Kings 18:20-24)

Who decides you or God?

Today there is an overwhelming role reversal going on, husband and wife, children and parents, it's even evident in the schools, Christians and sinners, yes, often our lives are dirty, some as dirty as the sinners.

We have house parties, we gamble, exercising trying to get rich quick schemes, again Christians acting just like sinners, difference is that the sinner is just doing what the sinner does.

We go to God with our petty orders, we have changed so much with this role-playing that we have taken God out of His rightful place in our lives.

King Ahab was the boldest king that ever lived; he made his daddy look like a joke.

You need to be very careful of who you marry; because you just may be marrying a Jezebel, most Christians are really not spiritually matched up, because God had nothing to do with it, that is why you feel that you can do as you please, you may think that you are getting by, but you are not.

God does get tired of your mess, and He will get your attention at one point or another.

Sin has a way of drying a Christian out; you can't praise God because you are in your sins, it makes you shame, it speaks to you, and it tells you to get somewhere and sit down, when you ought to be giving the ultimate praise.

God feeds him (1 Kings 17), He knows how to give you another brook, God sent him to the woman to eat and be fed.

This was the episode of Elijah and the power of prayer, you can't serve over here and run over there, you have to walk in your proper place.

Do you want to stay in sin? I pray not, brothers and sisters, you have got to make a choice; you cannot have it your way, because God is not Burger King, you know, you choose, and digest as you please.

You cannot run your life; and let God run it too, you have to be willing to crucify self, step back, and let God be God.

Let God reign in your life; you will be much better off, there is no way that you can be a luke warm Christian and please the Father.

You have got to allow God to move back into His proper place; that is in your heart.

The way to come out of your drought is to exercise the power within, because the power is in the one that you trust, and pray to.

# Good Attitude No Matter What

(2 Corinthians 4:17)

Blessings will endure forever.

It's very easy to praise God for a new car, job, house, etc, but what about when you have nothing? There is still a certain way that a Christian ought to carry themselves.

We also need to understand that we are going to have problems; no matter where we go, or what we do; trouble just has a way of finding you.

No problem comes into your life by accident, if it's there, then it is because God has allowed it; and wills it to be so.

Nothing happens to you without His knowledge, For example God brought Job's name up, and God removed the hedge of protection from around him.

It is time that you learn a lesson from your problems.

A good attitude is required of believers, not a select few but all believers.

You have to know that when you go through, you do not go through alone, to God be the glory.

God's Word lets us know that it rains on the just as well as the unjust, Scripture calls it your light affliction, for every person the size of the affliction is different, and you do need to thank God for it being light.

Aren't you glad that God knows how much you can take; it is minimal it is also momentary, your affliction is made just for you, it will work for you, and it is also meaningful?

Pray and ask God to help you learn from it, surely He will do what no one else can, for you, and with you.

When God teaches you, you have been thoroughly taught.

Then you can in gratitude to the Father, help someone else to understand; that there are some things that we must and will go through, after all He certainly knows what is best for His children, wouldn't you agree? Oh, I know you do, praise is to God, Amen.

## The Lord's Priorities

(Hosea 6:6)

Should be first and foremost

Mercy is to be desired, God gives us a brand new mercy every day; mercy follows us as we follow Christ.

You should have a grateful heart, spirit, and mind, because the Lord has also given us knowledge, and it is ours for the taking.

But there is one thing that we all must do, and that is to seek Him in His holy Word.

It's really amazing how Christians do things from day to day that is not in God's will. Yet they are never moved by it, it does not bother them at all, but it should make you very nervous to just do things contrary to the will of God; that is a dangerous thing, you need to have a repentant heart.

Thank God for mercy, God is so good to us that He gives us chances each and every day to change for the better, (Have you changed)?

Does it bother you when you do things that you shouldn't? This is just a thought, but a good one I must say.

If you are a born again Christian you must find your way back to God, because until you do you will have spiritual unrest. God said if we do this, then He would heal us, (Hosea 6:1).

Sometime we want to blame Satan, and give him credit for all the wrong things that go on in our lives; well you are wrong, some things are God ordained to train us and get us into position to be used by Him.

You have the Holy Ghost living in you; why not let Him have His way?

When you allow Him to move in your life He does just that.

We get ourselves into predicaments, and it takes us days to get out, if ever, but God can do it in seconds, minutes, hours, or days, it is always up to Him as to how long we are to stay in something, it may even take years.

You should put God first in your life, even above yourself, He is always true to His Word and He never fails.

Getting to know Him should be first and foremost, examine your life and see where it is that He fits and what place is He in?

Only you hold that answer, be honest with yourself, and reorganize today, I assure you it will be life changing.

# Are You Standing?

(1 Corinthians 10:12-13)

Watch out now

Some time we can get too confident in our thinking, the very time I think that I am alright that is when I am not, so does not trust your own fleshly thoughts because they only lead to destruction, and they get in the way of what the Holy Ghost is trying to do in and through you.

For instance have you ever got bogged down in your thinking? What you are going to do about this, and how are you going to take care of that.

This is how temptation gets us to move into areas of trying to do things we cannot.

The only way to solve your problem or concern is by going to the Lord in prayer and waiting on your answer to come from Him.

I know from experience it is not an easy thing to do, there have been times when I prayed and got up with my own solution, let me tell you it does not work; as a matter of fact it only makes things worse.

The only way that we will be able to stand in any of our everyday situations is by putting our trust in God; He is faithful to deliver you out of whatever it may be in His own time.

I know that even now some are suffering financially, some from the loss of a job, some maybe even the loss of a loved one, and on and on.

But I say to you, He is the answer to all of your troubles.

He has given us that someone who is able to see us through anything and everything, even in your temptation He has provided you a way out.

Some people may have to endure longer than others, but He is still the way out.

Just know that He loves you and cares for you.

When you begin to accept the Lord totally in your life and believe on Him, things will change for the better.

Then you truly will stand, because He will be holding you up, (verse 12). Therefore let him who thinks he stands take heed that he does not fall. (Verse 13) No temptation has overtaken you but such as is common to man; and God is faithful, who will not allow you to be tempted beyond what you are able, but with the temptation will provide the way of escape also, so that you will be able to endure it.

## I AM WHO I AM

(Exodus 3:14)

Has sent me to you

What an Awesome God we serve, God called you the same as He called Moses; and it is up to you as to whether or not you will obey, because He will not force you to do anything. It is a blessing to be called into the work of the Lord.

Don't you hear His still small voice calling out to you? He is saying come to me that I may use you today, what will your reply be back to Him? What excuse do you have for Him today? What are you allowing to take His place today? Do you really know Him?

I know these are some very potent questions; they are before you for a very good reason, they are to make you think, they should keep you pretty busy searching within yourself. When you look within, you will find answers to all of these.

Moses had questions and He asked them, that is all you have to do, if you ask, God will give you the answers.

You may be the one that gets delivered today, if you are serious about your Christian walk with the Lord.

God has commissioned His people to do great works, but some Christians do not feel that their calling is important, well it is, it may not be that calling that stands out for everyone to see, but, important it is, some person's life is depending on your accepting your holy commission.

It is not enough that you have been saved, to just keep it within yourself, go back, and get somebody else.

But how can you when you don't know how or who it is that is sending you?

Your Father has a name that is greater than any name, in the earth, or in the heavens, or in the world below.

When you go, and you will, let those that He is sending you to know that the Great I AM has sent you, it is an honor and a pleasure to be sent by God, and it is a real blessing to bring out another soul from the world of sin and death, into everlasting life.

## False Advertisement

(St. Matthew 21:19)

It's the in thing

Most things advertised today are not what they are made out to be, nothing is as good as it looks, and most people do not find this out until after they have made their purchase.

We buy for some of the craziest reasons one being designer names, we go to the big name stores verses the cheaper ones.

We like it fake, and we like it big, well you are representing a name that is above every name, but how do you treat it? Are you a false advertiser?

You should be very careful of how you carry the name Christian; someone is watching you.

The Golden rule tells us to love our neighbor as ourselves, yet you find this hard to do.

When things or people let you down what kind of commercial do you run? Is it one that people would come back to see, or is it one that turns everyone off?

As a child of God you have to be a good representative, because after all it is not about you.

Your Father (God) is The King of Kings; and Lord of Lord's, if things are a letdown to you, what do you think you are doing to the Lord.

When you don't obey, you are just that, a letdown.

What got this tree in trouble? It was professing something it did not possess; it indicated that it had figs, because it had leaves first, we are just like that tree; we make false promises that we cannot perform.

We look full, and we are, but what we are full of is air.

There is a real danger in false advertisement, because there is no warranty.

As a Christian I must live life to its fullest in the Lord, then my life will in turn produce the fruit that is within me, and it is all because of my obedience to the Lord God Almighty.

## Just A Reminder

(James 1:2-3)

He sure knows

God knows what we need, but every time we get ready to do something here comes trouble, so in these dark times we have to learn what to do.

Our trials should be faced with an attitude of joy and peace of mind, you just can't worry about folks lying on you, there are many other things that happen to us in a day's time, but we have to face them, then let go and let God have His way.

Truth is if you did not you would lose your mind; we must learn how to conduct ourselves.

We must praise God all the time; in our circumstances and conditions, you don't have to let trouble control you, and your life.

This was not directed to any particular group, it was to be read and passed on.

Paul said my brother count it all joy, we are the ones that have much to be joyful about.

The number one thing to be joyful for is that He saved you from a burning hell.

I must say that this does not apply to you, if you do not have Jesus in your life, because if you don't have Him (Jesus Christ), you certainly don't have anything to be happy about.

But, you do have something to be found out, you must come to know the Lord for yourself, then you can and will have a right to be the chief of your joy, because God gave you charge over that.

So, if you are unhappy for whatever reason it is up to you to change it, because you do have the power and you should be in control.

Paul also talks about divers, meaning a whole lot; we will be tried and tested but you have the Lord to go through with you, and you should come through as gold.

 If you do not have the joy of the Lord in your heart, call it forth today, because it is yours for the receiving; now read James, and let it saturate you.

# Great Cloud Of Witnesses

(Hebrews 12:1)

Stay in the race

A lot of people start out running; it's not good to just start. What are you running for?

Some people run for health reasons, others run because of the loss of a loved one, or they themselves have been in a battle with some disease such as cancer, heart attack, diabetes, etc. these are just some of the reasons people run.

But there is another race before all mankind it is the race of Christianity.

What we need to do is get instructions as to how we are to run, because if we don't we will be all over the place.

When you have instructions you will run a proper race, and you will do it according to the orders placed before you, yes there is a proper way to run.

The Word of God teaches us this, if I am running according to His will I will not easily tire out or give up; I will be able to hold out and see what the end is going to be.

Have you ever watched as some people ran a good Christian race, well, if they can do it you certainly can?

The author here talks about a great cloud of witnesses; that should and ought to include you and me, are you a witness for the Lord?

Reading the Word prepares me for my run, you do know that we all have our own race to complete, our own course to run.

If you are going to run this race you have to be a citizen of the Kingdom of God, you cannot receive your crown any other way.

When you entered a race you had to be there for at least ten months, you had to be on a strict diet, one reason many Christian cannot run freely is because they are eating from too many different tables.

You need to get where God has placed you and let the Angel of the church feed you (the Pastor); you will never be able to run if you are constantly moving around.

Regardless of what they did they all had the same training (the athletes of that day) the same applies to us; you have to be trained in order to run a good race.

Regardless of the job descriptions, there were no amateurs. Either you are or you are not.

They had Greek god's; and they were running to please them, we have God the Father, God the Son, and God the Holy Ghost, Now run to please Him, and for no other reason.

He also talks about weight and sin as though they are two different things, there are some things that can really mess up your running, but they got down to the bare necessities, they trained and raced naked, they trained in heavy boots, and you had to drop the weight at the right time, you have to know when to put things in their right perspective.

Priority is in order, when you put things before the Lord they become a weight, but sin is anything that goes against the will and ways of God.

# I Still Remember

(St. Luke 17:11-19)

Thank you Lord

As Christians some of us can have some awfully bad manners, yes I said it, God blesses and you never say thank you, duly noted I did say some.

Jesus healed all ten lepers and what happened? Only one of them came back and glorified Him. Jesus was a stranger, and it seems somewhat odd, that someone who did not know Him had returned to say thanks.

In (verse 13), they were all speaking to Jesus and asking for His mercy, Jesus had compassion on these men; and His response was, "go" and show yourselves to the priest.

Can you see it; even though Jesus blesses them there is something they had to do in order to receive it?

We have to be obedient to His every word, we have to have faith, because what He tells us shall come to past; He is God, and He cannot lie.

Lepers could not be around other people, and yet they managed to get to the Lord, it is somewhat the same with us, if you are sin sick, you certainly do possess a form of leprosy.

There is only one healer, Jesus is His name, and you must call upon Him, to heal and change you, because He is the only one who can and will.

Go ahead and be like this one leper, he recognized his blessing; he also realized that he needed Jesus.

If you plan on making it from this world to the next you have got to be led by Him, not part of the way, but all of the way.

If you have not taken the time to bless Him for His goodness and mercy today this would be a good place to stop and do it.

This would be the third and final act of the leper, the facts are that he returned to give thanks to the Lord Jesus Christ; yes, He is worthy to be praised; and He is worthy to be remembered, Amen.

# Let The Word Work In You

(2 Timothy 3:16)

You will grow if you do

The Word of God is powerful, and there is power in this scripture, the Word is so needed today.

These words were written to encourage Timothy, by Paul, they are also here to encourage us, because in the last days things will be so perilous. The Lord has mercy and we are already there. Where is there?

Where men have become lovers of themselves, these things are not at all natural; people believe what they want to believe, and they call themselves Christians, Christian means to be Christ like.

I believe the unadulterated Word of God, the Bible is the only book that speaks the real truth for all mankind, the Bible is a giant compared to other books.

Whatever has been and is written in any form or fashion has extended itself from the Bible.

Man's views do not amount to a hill of beans; what lies ahead for us all is found in the holy pages of the Word of God, everything that you need is there, the problem is that man has become stagnate and refuses to read it.

One thing that I know for sure is that if you ever decide to read it, and I pray you will, it will certainly and without a doubt change you, you will never be the same, if you let the Word move in; because it is life changing.

It is not a book to be toyed or played with; it is Jesus Christ; Savior and Redeemer.

It is a dangerous thing to try and change it to fit your lifestyle, if you are wrong, then you are wrong.

He tells us that every one that does this, to him all of the plagues will be added, and your name will be taken out of the book, (Revelation 22:18-19).

It is time that you made the right choice, and that is to live according to His holy Word; God's Word is a living Word.

The choice is yours, what will it be for you, heaven or hell.

God controlled these authors; now that you know that the Word is used for your Christian growth let God have His way in your life.

God will fix you up (Galatians 5:1), He tells us to not be entangled again with the yoke of bondage, you have been loosed from it, don't return again, you are free and playtime is over.

# Don't Wait Until You Are In Hell To Get It Right

(St. Luke 16:19-39)

It won't work

We don't know when Jesus is going to come back, so you need to be working on getting right every day that you have; don't wait until it is too late to do it.

This is the only time that you are going to have, right now, this very present moment.

Hell is certainly real, for those of you who may be reading this and have some doubts, well; doubt no more.

It is thinking and decision time on your part, if you are not saved, get saved today, and if you know someone who is not saved and you are, lead them to Christ, if you don't know how; get them to someone who does.

It is imperative that all men have an opportunity to be saved; this certainly is not hell even though sometimes it may feel that way to you, believe me, it is not, this is just a foretaste of things to come.

God has told us there is a hell, Jesus has told us there is a hell, and the Holy Ghost is trying to keep us from going to hell. I do not want any part of hell, and I pray you do not either.

This rich man's fault was just that, his richness, it does not matter how much money you have, you need Jesus, money cannot save you.

Another thing about the rich man is that he died; your money cannot stop death, you will die one day. This is our common ground every man, woman, boy, and girl has to die, and will die, nothing in this world can stop that, he is coming (death).

The poor man and the rich man had a common ground; the poor man was at his gate. There is somebody at your gate, what are you going to do about it? God has said to us we are to care for one another, if you are hungry, God said to feed you, if you are naked, God said to give you clothes.

Don't get caught up because you have plenty and someone else does not, you have for the simple reason of giving. But what are you doing with your crumbs? Please don't let them send you to hell.

It is a sad thing that two people cannot treat each other right, but can treat their pets like kings and queens; and that is far better than you treat one another.

The dog was better to him than the rich man, he bought him comfort (he licked his sores), and he showed more caring than the rich man did.

There are some things that will go with you when you die; your feelings go with you, and your conscience goes with you, yes, you will know exactly where you are.

Don't be like the rich man, he waited until he was in hell to pray, he had feelings, he got thirsty, he had knowledge of where he was and what he wanted to do for those he left behind. The sad thing about this is that no warning can come from hell to those you leave behind, they have the same opportunity that you do, the Word is going forth, and it is being taught, the Word is Jesus Christ our Lord and Savior!

## Too Sleepy To Pray

(St. Matthew 26:36-45)

Tell the truth shame the devil

Two gardens: the Garden of Eden, and the Garden of Gethsemane. The first garden was the downfall, which was Adam. The second was Jesus Christ. Gethsemane means; all pressed.

Jesus had an inner circle, He told them for this cause I came into the world, yes Jesus knew what He had come to do.

There were four men in the garden; others were Peter, James, and John.

Jesus Christ was and is the sin bearer for all mankind.

The sleep of a laboring man is sweet, but it is dangerous to sleep at the wrong time. For example: when you ought to be praying you are asleep, sound familiar.

Most of us just don't take the time to pray, but we find time to do everything else; and stay wide-awake while doing it.

We go to work and stay awake, no matter what time of day or night; we manage to stay wide awake.

A lot of Christian's sleep doing sermon time, with their eyes wide open; they cannot tell you one thing that the Pastor has said, and sure enough, do not ask what the sermon topic was; the answer will be a whopping I don't remember, okay.

Where do you fit in this; are you napping, or are you all the way gone? If you choose either of these you need help. There's nothing that goes on inside of you that Jesus can't change. When we sleep without our covering it leaves room for the enemy to come in, every time Jesus came back to His disciples He found them sleeping, His question to them was can you not stay awake for one hour.

He came to them three times, the last time He told them to take their rest, what is He telling you? What are you saying back to Him? Are you watching or are you asleep?

Jesus is waiting on you to give it to Him, and He desires our total attention, because your life depends on it.

Jesus Christ did not die in vain, I know this to be true because I' am a living witnesses of what He can and will do, what about you?

# Lost But Still Valuable

(St. Luke 15:8-10)

He cherishes you

Everywhere Jesus was a crowd showed up. You have right now to get ready to go home, or somewhere. Our destination is left up to us. Jesus prayed fifteen different prayers, and St. Luke records eleven of those.

He entered the house to break bread; people will be saved when those of us who are, go out among those who are not.

Jesus did it, and He did it without participating in what they were doing.

Chapter fifteen talks about a sheep that could not see and wandered off, it also talks about the woman and the search for the coin that was lost in the house. We too need to do a thorough search; she did not give up until she found the lost coin.

It did not matter to her that she had nine left, the coin was silver; which lets us know that it was valuable; silver represents the soul.

Every soul is worth something, there are even people in the church that are lost; and, we should never give up on anyone.

 If you know someone that is in this state go and remind him or her to not give up; being lost in the house is not a bad thing, because you are still valuable, (verse 8). The candle represents (St. John 1) "The Word is" Jesus.

You need to get Him inside of you, because that is when the light will shine, you see He is the light (St. Matthew

5:16) tells us to let your light so shine, people need to see the real you they need to see what you are doing, so let the Word live in you.

Even though the coin was out of place it was still valuable, meaning you or someone you know.

A lot of Christians are out of place but they are still valuable.

Some of us have fell into the wrong hands, now that you know, it is time to get back to where you belong, in the right hands, doing the right things.

That is the only way you will ever be able to lead someone else to Christ,

The Potter is waiting to mold and make you again, now be willing to let Him have His way with you.

# Good Recipe For Wisdom

(St. Matthew 2:1)

God's Awesome Wisdom

Wisdom comes from God. There are some folk who do foolish things, and they are not all children. If you are a Christian and have not gotten any wiser then you are still doing stupid things. The purpose of Matthew's gospel is to present Him asking of the Jews.

A real wise person is one who wants to get to Jesus, (v 3 and 10).

They followed the right star; many of us follow our own stars, for instance; professional ball players, professional golfers and others.

Instead of following a star as a Christian I should be leading for someone else, (St. Matthew 5:16) we really do have to let our light shine.

They followed His star, it took them to Jesus, if you are going to lead make sure that your leading stops at Jesus.

I certainly would not want to lead anyone anywhere else but to Jesus Christ our Lord. Where are you leading and who is it that is following you? You do know that someone is watching your every move?

They had a desire to see Jesus, so they followed the star; they thanked God for the star. You should be thanking God for the star that led you to Him.

When they got there they had enough sense to go in (2:11), when you get to the house of God have enough sense to go in, because what you need is on the inside.

They had enough sense to know what to do when they saw Him, if you don't know what to do when you go before Him let me help you, bow down and worship Him, praise and honor Him. They did not just worship Him, they fell down and worshipped Him; do not be ashamed to praise God who gave you life and breath.

Most Christians are not ashamed to do the other things that they do, and they do not have to be primed and pumped to do what they do. They just do it because it comes natural. Well if you come around Jesus enough, that who is spiritual; will become the norm for you, then you will be on your way praising and adoring the Lord.

It will not matter to you who sees you, or who knows you, all that will be important to you is to praise His Holy Name.

When you come humble before the Lord things happen, your worship will be intentional; you will look forward to coming into His house to give Him praise, you will lift up holy hands in the sanctuary, and you will present your gifts in the tithe and the offering willingly and without being asked too.

They did all of this they gave gifts, they lifted their hands in praise, and they opened their pockets. Why? Because they realized who He was, and they knew that He was worthy of all they presented and more, He is Jesus, He is Lord, and He is Savior, Praise Him today.

## Leaving Better

(St. Luke 13:10-13)

The Word will get you there

Wouldn't it be nice if all the churches of God that come together Sunday after Sunday, and Wednesday after Wednesday, and whatever time they meet, left out of the sanctuary better than they came? I think you know the answer to this.

It is very possible to do so, but you must pay attention to the Word of God in order to achieve this. When Jesus is in the house it is very important that you give Him your undivided attention.

Some people do not meet Him until on Sunday's or Wednesday's; and even then they have the nerve to ignore parts of what He is saying to them.

I challenge you today to not be satisfied with where you are in Christ, because when you come looking and ready to listen; you will receive, and when you receive the Lord God this will bring about a miraculous change in you.

I give God the glory, the honor, and the praise, for His Awesome works.

No one should ever get your attention in the sanctuary but the Lord, you must know that when you enter the house of God that there is another present to deter you from your blessings.

The devil comes to the meeting too, he gets a ride every Sunday with someone.

Look at the scripture in this subject; the woman came crooked but she left straight, you must be determined that what you come for, you will not leave, until you have received it.

You cannot fix your affliction but you have put yourself in a position for it to be removed, if you will just pay attention, apply what you hear, and then trust the Lord, to bring you out, because can't nobody do it like Jesus?

You may come looking like sin but you can leave healed of the sin, we are past the time of looking like sin; Christian brothers and sisters it is time you started to look like the one who has called you out.

If you are going to ever help someone else, stop concentrating on doing things in your own will that does not work, and start letting go and letting God have His way. The woman had her affliction for eighteen years, how long have you had yours?

Some of us don't have an upward look, (v.16) Satan had her, but through it all; she had sense enough to get to Jesus. When Jesus saw her, He called her, and healed her. His words were; woman you have been loosed. Then she was freed of her affliction, what about you? Once the Lord frees you; don't you turn back?

# Putting The Word Into Action

(James 1:25)

To do is divine

It seems that the Bible is just a part of our wardrobe; because we have in our mind there is certain attire for us coming to church.

The Word is more than just to be quoted or learned. James is the oldest half brother of Jesus Christ. James recognized the need for gentiles to be saved, so he writes a circular letter to be read and passed on, in this first Chapter he is writing to the Jews that had gone outside of Jerusalem.

The Word of God is so Awesome, that He has gotten us of His own Self-will, we are His off spring.

The Word is to be probed into; but we keep glancing at it, we have got to get down into it, in order to understand.

This is the only book that the Author is willing to show up in.

We keep forsaking and forfeiting our privilege to meet with Him, when He has opened the way. Jesus died on the cross at Calvary, and the curtain was torn into from top to bottom, therefore making a way for you and me.

The law says you will do right because you want to do right.

We have liberty (freedom) therefore we need to change our appetites. The Word is to be practiced, even a sinner knows the Word, and you can know it and still sin, just like the devil. After all there are Christians doing it every day, if you would just do the part of the Word that you already know that would be enough to keep you busy.

We as Christians should demonstrate it, okay; I ought to be seen working and doing God's will.

Question is where would your life lead me if it were my only Bible? What would it teach me? What would I learn? Would I end up in heaven or hell?

Can you tell the sinner man "read me, and I will show you how to run when you don't feel like running"?

Now, get down into the Word and see for yourself, let Jesus take you there, and be truly born again, and when you get into it preserve it; then find yourself where He desires you to be. Keep it, hold on to it, and remember what you studied. Then you will become that changed person in Him.

# The Other Side Of Midnight

(Psalms 30:5)

Day light is coming

No matter what you are going through if you would just wait, hold on, and trust in God things will get better for you.

There are those who will not wait on the Lord, and they are trying to do things on their own, this only makes it worse.

The devil brings many storms, and he will speak to you when you are in hard times, or in some type of depression, but as a child of God you have no business letting those thoughts get you down or control you.

As a matter of fact you should not even entertain the things that the enemy is bringing to your mind. You see it is his desire to kill you, he's not playing, he is for real in everything that he does, or tries to do in your life, now cast him down in the name of Jesus.

There is always a word from the Lord for everything we go through; there is nothing that He cannot help us to change or solve. If you are going through let the Lord have it, I guarantee you that He can do much more with it than you ever will or can.

If you have thoughts of committing suicide, don't. Know that Jesus is ever present in your life, the key to it all is letting Him have his way. I know that you are tired of trying to fight and solve your own problems, aren't we all?

Let Jesus have it right now, today, right where you are at this very moment turn it over to the Lord.

Truly, truly, and without a doubt on one side of your life there is midnight, but if you would just look to the other side then you will see life, a life that is worth living, a life that is going to last forever and ever, and now we thank you, Lord; today for teaching us how to wait on you, Amen.

## The Purpose Of The Word

(2 Timothy 3:16)

It comes directly from God

When we learn what the purpose of the Word is, then we can apply it. The Word is not designated to make you shout on Sunday and live any kind of way the rest of the week.

There are those who would like to change it to fit them and what they do, but it won't work.

The Bible tells us that all scripture is God breathed, anything that is said is to be backed by His holy Word. The Word is given by the inspiration of the Holy Ghost.

Yes there are some days when we are not fond of each other and we may want to do things our way, but the Word of God is still to be obeyed.

We do what we do because our commitment is to God, and for no other reason.

These men who penned the Word were not the authors they were just simply doing what God had called them to do. The Author is the Holy Ghost.

God did not intend for us to understand our carnal mind from a child (verse 15).

There are a lot of religious things you can read, but none of it comes up to the standard of the Word, the Word is profitable, it's good for you, you gain from the reading of the Word; and you grow from the reading of the Word.

If the Word does not come first in your life then you are not where you ought to be, the Word lets you know what is right and what is not.

Does His Word come first in your life? If not you are just in the realm of a social club religion, Oh God, help.

The Word is good for teaching, are you teachable? Teaching must be practiced, you cannot make God's Word fit your doctrine, it will not work; you need to make sure that your doctrine is lining up with His Word.

A lot of Churches and the Christians are getting away from this, you want to do it like the others are doing it, well if God did not ordain something for His house leave it alone, and let Him show you what He wants, for His house.

The Word is good for reproof; your church should be a Bible based covenant church after all it is God's house, not yours.

The Word is good for rebuke; to correct you, and make you better; its purpose is also to drive you to correction. You see it will replace your wrong action with correct ones, if you allow it to. It does me no good to put down wrong, if I am not going to pick up right. It tells us how to do the right things, and to live what you know. It's good for instructions in righteousness. The true church says now if the Word says it, then we are going to do it, and the reason is, because it comes directly from God.

## Do It

(St. John 2:1-11)

God said it

The real purpose of the Word has been overlooked so long. In response to the Word we ought to have a Nike religion; that is not to change it or dissect it.

We should say if it is in the Word whether I like it or not I am going to do it.

True there are parts of the "Word" we do not like, for instance His Word says Love your enemies, but do you? It also says give, but do you? It tells us to bring our tithes and offerings, but do you?

I know right now you are ready to stop reading just because of the conviction you feel in your spirit, but I encourage you to keep on going.

His Word says no sex before marriage, but you do?

Now get this; we have not been called to like His Word, we have been called to just do what it says.

Obey, because obedience is better than sacrifice, it is time for you to get up under the will of your Father, and be delivered today, receive your miracle.

Jesus followed the instructions of His Father, even though Mary asks of Him, it was now time to do His Father's holy will.

We need to learn how to do, not because of what mother said (verse 4).

We have got to have confidence in His Word, whatever the Lord is saying do it.

I am a living witness you will be blessed for it, Mary is saying today when you do, do it with confidence.

(Verse 6) There were six water pots in that day made of clay; only the ones Jesus used were made of stone.

When water was in the clay pots it would wind up dirty because of the moving around in the pots, Jesus is saying to you, whatever I give you, I don't want it tainted by the things of the world, the church is not to copy the things of this world, you are the Church, you are who He is speaking too.

Jesus needs containers that will not mix others things with what He puts inside.

In that day it was normally the women who carried the pots, but Jesus told the men to carry them. It was not a time for debate, Jesus had spoken and it was simply time to obey. Obedience will get the job done; you do not have to pray for what to do when you already know what is to be done, just do it.

## The Sanctuary

(St. Luke 15:25-32)

It belongs to God

Luke was the beloved physician he presents the Lord as the Son of man. John presents Him as the Son of God.

These sheep are somewhat different than the sheep of today; all sheep need the Shepherd, even though they may feel they don't.

They did not get mad and fall out with the Shepherd, and many today do not intend to do so either, but gradually, you have dropped all the way out of the house of God.

The coin just dropped off, it was in the house, but lost; some Christians are the same way, they are in the house of God one week, and out the next. Have you ever asked yourself why? It is very dangerous when we start to act in this manner, and if you continue to do this you start to thinking and believing that you can take care of yourself, when you know that you cannot.

If you are a born-again Christian you know without a shadow of a doubt that you need the Lord.

The earthly Father's house does in a way represent the Church, some who are in the church act in ways that they should not.

We must respect God's house, there are some things that you just should not do in His house. His house is the house of prayer.

The gossiping and back biting has no place in it, even though it's very much present; the change has to be made on the inside of you, and that change has to be in your heart.

We are to share the Good News; but we cannot do this if we are not in the house to receive it, how can you share what you have not heard?

A true servant chooses to tell the good things over the bad, what servant are you? The prodigal son came home and his brother got jealous, and angry.

Our job when someone comes home is not to be jealous or angry but to rejoice, it does not matter what you know about them, don't you know that somebody knows something about you, so now that you have regained your senses rejoice, because one day grace and mercy found you, and the same way that grace and mercy found you, they are still seeking and finding others.

Remember we are all here by the grace of God, so give praise to His holy name.

I' am reminded of the scripture that tells us we have all sinned and fallen short of the glory of God, that's enough to keep me in my place, what about you? I will rejoice for my brothers and my sisters; that are still coming home.

## Our Job

(2 Timothy 4:1-8)

May your will be done in us

There are jobs to be done, the job of the Pastor is to make sure that the Word of God goes forth, there is another job that we are all responsible for; it is making sure that people know who Jesus is and that souls are saved.

Paul wrote this while he was in prison, in the inner most part, the dungeon, he wrote it to his beloved son in the gospel, Timothy.

He wrote this encouraging letter to his son who was sick; he gives him a stern charge, which is to preach the gospel.

His job as a preacher was to relate the Word to others and to do it right, there was to be no changing of the Word.

But now we see it happening today where some preachers are changing the Word of God to please those they are preaching too, and to keep their status in the church that they are shepherding in, and also to be liked by those who are financially fit.

This is a very dangerous thing to do (Revelation 1:18-19. 22:18-19), if you are a Pastor or teacher I admonish you today to preach the Word the way that God would have it done. Don't worry about what man will say to you, or do to you, because God is greater, and He is the one that you should be most concerned about pleasing.

Timothy had a timid spirit, a lot of Christians have this same spirit; and it does not come from God.

When you try keeping up with all the different movements you will be timid, wait on God and let Him lead you. Be consistent in your work for the Lord, he told him to preach in season and out (meaning at all times), the Word is to be preached and heard.

The Word of God will show you the right way to do whatever it is that He is calling you to do, this is where reproof comes in; you should be able to see the error of your ways.

When you are rebuked and chastised that is the time to give up your sins, some things should not be allowed to grow, always address your issues.

The message of the gospel should keep you lifted up, because it adds an element of hope to every bad situation.

The truth may be that you are on your way to hell, but the gospel lets you know you can be saved.

Most definitely, lives should change because of the Word of God, so be patient in your walk, and keep the Word of God ever before you, it is your strength and He is your source.

# Balanced In Your Belief

(St. John 12:1-3)

You can be just that

It is not good enough to just be a member in the church; you have to grow up from when you first came.

Most people want to talk about when they came, well I ask you what about now?

Jesus left but now He's back; we have to do the same exact thing.

I believe that this is touching someone right now, right where you are.

We have to go back to our family members, and to others, and we must keep going back, we find Jesus back in Bethany.

Jesus was at the house of Lazarus, one whom He had just raised from the dead; Lazarus had already begun to stink.

It is imperative that we get it together, it's not about us, but it is about Kingdom building, we cannot do it with a stinking lifestyle and a stinking attitude.

The way we talk, live, and act, our motives and all of this has to change when we began to live our lives for the Lord.

There are a lot of unbalanced Christians, but you must know that if you want something to change, it begins first with you.

The same as it was with Lazarus, only Jesus could raise Him up, and He is the only one that can do it for you.

Now if you have been depending on others, let go, and let Him have control in your life.

Aren't you tired? Haven't you made a big enough mess of things? If you are not walking with the Lord then you are dead, yes, dead in your sins, it's time to let Him raise you, the same way that He called out to Lazarus, He is calling out to you, can't you hear Him calling your name _____.

When you come into total obedience, it brings joy into your life, both physically and spiritually, so you rejoice. Praise Him, and remember; there is always going to be someone who needs to be where you are now, why not go back and get him or her? Then the Father will be pleased with you.

# Don't Mistake Delay For Denial

(St. John 11:1-6

He will be there

A lot of times it may seem as though The Lord God has forgotten you, or that He is not coming to see about you, but He has not, all you have to do is wait on Him.

God does not move according to our timing, as a matter of fact His timing is nothing like ours, I cannot command God to come, and He comes, Our Father moves according to His holy will.

We have to trust Him and hold on to our faith.

I know this for a fact, I may want Him to come right now, but His right now maybe three years, or two days from now which is nothing to God.

But what are you going to do in the meantime? Will you wait on Him? We only make things worse when we attempt to fix it.

Look at His past record, He never fails, He made us, and He knows exactly what we can and cannot do.

If the devil is not bothering you, and everything is just lovely; that only means that you are not doing anything. You probably are in the same line with him, I assure you; that when you start doing something right he is coming, (Satan).

The Lord tells us that we will be persecuted for His sake, so, if you are going through in Jesus name just hold on, help is on the way.

The Lord God does not forsake His own.

This was a well- loved family, it really does hurt to see a love one sick, as a matter of fact; their affliction becomes ours.

Even when you are a close friend to someone else, you should be able to feel his or her pain. The blessing to is: that, the Lord assures us; that all sickness is not unto death, Hallelujah, aren't you glad? That should be joy to you.

They were separated from Jesus only by a day and a half, how far away from the Lord are you? If you would get in His Word, then there will be a lot of things that will not over take you, the way that they have overtaken you in the past. Things took you then because you had nothing to fall back on and no arms to fall into; so, turn it over to the Lord and trust Him to bring you through, He can, and He will.

# Don't Lose Your Fire

(Revelation 2:1-5)

To be an effective servant you must have time to set and to serve. As Christians we do get to a point in our spiritual walk where our fire goes to dwindling.

Do you remember how you were when you first came to Christ? Everything was so exciting to you, nothing could mess you up, you wanted to have a hand in everything and you felt slighted when you were not asked to do something. Well what about now? What happened to you? The work is still there.

The Lord still needs dedicated Christians who will do and not complain maybe if you would just reflect back on how He saved you, died for you, and bought you out, there would be no room for that other stuff. As a matter of fact, you should feel somewhat sad, if you have done this, but, don't stay there, get up, and get busy in Jesus.

Because He cares for you, He loves you; and He does not hold grudges.

Each letter was written to address a specific need that the church was faced with; Christ has given each church what she needs, and if you are there, then you are a part of that.

Find out what it is that He wants you to do and get busy, its fun working for Jesus.

There is still a lot of work to be done before the Lord makes His entrance. I would really hate to be caught sitting down on Him. We have this I' am going to let them do it attitude, well that does not make it right; He needs you too.

My pastor has taught us that you are a part of the puzzle, and if you are missing, it can never be totally put together; but with everyone in his or her proper place things will go according to schedule.

 So, don't you let it be said that you were the one that held up the progress of the house.

When He gets down to the reward He talks about the individual.

What will your reward be? He is warning the church, are you hearing him?

When He speaks we should definitely be paying attention, listen to what He is saying to you today; don't just blow it off like it is nothing.

Read it again and again, and pray; that He will help you get to where you need to be in His house.

# Prescription For A New Healthy Church

(1 Chronicles 7:14)

God is God

There is nothing that you can do to make God not be God, He is God, and you cannot add or take anything away from Him; He is who He is, "God".

There are a lot of disabled Christians; you must follow your prescription and take your medicine accordingly if you are to be well.

Don't you know that it is illegal to give your medicine to someone else? Even though there are many who are guilty of doing just that.

There are a lot of people in the church, but they are not all saved, including some of the members.

Jesus said, called by my name; this means not only saved but also separated from the world, and the ways of the world.

A lot of Christians are still striving to get there; some are still doing the same things that the sinners are doing.

Being a Christian means that you have got to be obedient; and learn how to walk in submission to the will of God, when you are disobedient you will fall.

Be very careful of where you fall from, because if you are going to fall, and you will, fall from your knees.

You have got to turn and you have got to surrender. God said my people.

He is also telling us what we are to turn from; God said your wicked ways.

 If you are one of those persons who thought you were better than someone who just came to Christ, just know that you are not, if you are one of those who have decided how a person should praise God saying they are too loud; just know that you don't have that right. It is time to stop the talking, as many of you are doing; it is time to really seek the Lord, with your whole heart.

# I Have Got Somewhere To Be

(Romans 8:28)

Get there in His power

Your calling goes beyond your salvation; that is not the place to say well I' am in, and I will now take a seat and wait on Jesus, wrong answer.

We have a divine call to destiny that was predestined before we were ever made.

I thank God for Salvation, it points us back to God; that is why it is so easy for some Christians to do nothing, but that should be a reason for us to do.

(Ephesians 2:10) says we are His workmanship, what Jesus did He meant to do, and now all we can do is walk in His will.

To be called is to be summoned by a higher power, a power that none of us possess, only Jesus Christ.

I heard God when He called me and I' am so glad that He did, I' am right where I desire to be, praising and serving Him.

God has to take us down before He brings us up, believe me, when I tell you that He will let you go through, it is a part of your growth process.

God has to take us out before He brings us in, He will allow us to do the things we desire to do, but the call does come. Be warned that if you get too far out, there is a possibility that you will not hear Him the way that you should; or either you will hear; and just not obey.

Don't be so quick to accept anything and anybody, that can be real trouble for you, you are playing with the devil when you start to do these kinds of things.

Nothing matters to you when you live out of His will; you won't care about anything or anyone, you will even lose yourself if you are not careful.

Turn around and let the Lord bless you, you will find that there is much safety in Him, you must be an over comer (verse 29), don't let the things that you go through, and have been through, get you down.

You see, God knew what you were going to do, even before you did it, nothing that we do amazes Him.

A word of caution; you are "Royalty", and you are His child, so without a doubt my friend; the best place and the safest place that you could ever be, is forever in the arms of the Master.

# How Much Do I Owe Him?

(Romans 12:1)

I cannot even begin to count

Jesus Christ died for us; He went through so much for us, He was beaten and slapped for us, they spit in His face for us, they mocked Him for us, and much, much, more.

He took care of our sins, and when they placed His back to the cross, He asked God to forgive them.

Jesus said and it is true, they know not what they do, do you know what you are doing?

Do you ever think about the things that I just mentioned above? I believe that if you did it would change your life drastically.

How much do you really owe Him? There is one thing that I do know, and it is this, you will never, ever, be able to repay the Lord for what He has done for you.

He said in this scripture I beseech you; meaning I beg of you, or I ask of you, it's your choice.

Jesus also calls you my brother; that's something to think about, He made it personal for everyone that has come, and will come back to Him.

Therefore tells us what to do with where we are, Mercy is an abundance of His mercy, and is brand new every morning; He loves us that much.

As kind as God is, nobody should have to prime you to praise and love Him.

Just knowing that He cried out on Calvary for me moves me to do all that I can while I possibly can for Him, because He is worthy of my praise, and He is worthy of yours too. I owe Him everything, yes; I should praise Him at all times; sick or well.

You should always be a witness in your praise, because someone needs to know that you know Him.

What would happen if some of your friends came to church with you, would they know you if they saw you in praise, or would they be in shock at what they are seeing? Can you praise Him, and not be ashamed of what others think about you? If not, you need to ask the Lord to help you get to that place in Him, yes, you do owe Him, and you can never repay Him, but, you can, and certainly you should, praise Him to the utmost, and give "The Lord" total praise.

## Do You Want To Get Well?

(St. John 5:1)

Jesus is the healer

You can look at some people and know right away that they are ill, and you may even have someone in your family that is ill or a friend that may be ill, have you ever thought about yourself being sick?

It does not matter how good you feel right now, just know there is something wrong with you.

I know by now you are thinking where in the world is this going? Let me get you out of suspense and into the real thing.

There is a disease called sin and you are sick with it, but, there is a remedy for your sickness, whose name is Jesus.

You can go to doctors all you want, but only He can heal you of this one.

Point is a lot of Christians do not want to get well, they enjoy living in sin, could it be that some even enjoy it as much as the sinner does?

In order to get well you need a healer, well, the Lord has sent one to you, to teach you, and help you grow, you have the Holy Ghost living inside of you, you have your Pastor / Teacher who brings healing words each Sunday and Wednesday, and you have the Word of God, the Bible that you can read, study, and meditate on for yourself.

How long have you been dealing with your disease? If you would be truthful with yourself it would probably add up to more than the sick man in this chapter, I 'am encouraging you too please read.

Thirty-eight years is a long time to be sick and depending on someone else to help you when you have all the help you need.

But He said "Lord I have no man to point me to the water" he was in the presence of the Lord, but could not see the healer standing before him.

Please Lord, have mercy on us; some of us are no different than he was.

Jesus is present with you, what more do you need?

Every appearance of Jesus was a lesson to humanity. Jesus' challenge to the man was for him to see where he was, or whether he wanted to get better.

Jesus wanted him to know that he was helpless, and He wanted him to focus, He wants the same for us, get your focus on the Lord for He is the one who has everything you need. The best thing that Jesus told him was to get up, He is telling you now, get up and walk; He wants you to have faith and trust in Him, whatever is holding you back just pick it up and get it out of your way.

When Jesus frees us, He wants us to let go of it; whatever it is. Aren't you tired of people carrying you? Jesus is giving you the ability to walk, now run and tell that, because somebody else really dose need to know.

# There Is A War Going On
(Ephesians 6:10)

We are under attack

We are at war and God is calling us to get our marching orders. We are trying to fight the devil with his weapons (Ephesians 6:12). Some in the church have gone "AWOL" this is a military term meaning; *away without leave.* But God is calling in your furlough. After all He did not give you permission to go.

We fight one another even though the fight is not really with man, Christians love covering stuff up, we love protecting wrong, we let too much go on in God's house.

In order to win a battle you have got to know whom you are fighting, and it is certainly and without a doubt not man, all though some treat it as such.

Some churches are taking people in and not teaching them anything, new members come and they go as fast as they come, Christians are still grouping themselves together, you have your own little circle of people, and it leaves no room for the new comers. A good soldier looks out for everyone; and if we are good soldiers our reputation will exceed us.

God left us His Word and that is all we need to fight with, we need to be great conduits. Paul was hooked up to the transformer; some of us are not hooked up to the right person, The Holy Ghost. When you get hooked up things begin to happen through you, and things will begin to change.

God is able to work His work through you, we need to utilize the power that God has given us; we have the power to pull down strongholds, we need to stay fervent in our prayer life and reading of the Word.

As soldiers of the Most High God too many of us have become cowards, where is your strength and why are you running from, instead of too? Answer is: you are not properly dressed.

There is something that we all need to do daily, (Ephesians 6:10-18) tells us to put on the whole armor of God, God will fight your battles, if you let Him; you should at this point be tired of fighting the enemy by yourself, you cannot win alone.

Our problem is that we are trying to fight a war that is Satanic; that war belongs to the Lord Jesus Christ. What Paul tells us to do is stand.

Somewhere between the first and second heaven there is a war going on, and all you need to do is stand still and see the works of the Lord.

## No Weapon Formed Will Prosper

(Isaiah 54:13-17)

No, no, no

No nation will ever again be allowed to defeat Israel; this will take place in the coming Millennial Kingdom, praise God.

I have complete trust in the Lord Jesus. Isaiah lets us know that God truly loves His people the Jews. I know that the same goes for you, and me, because we are His adopted children, therefore He loves us too.

He gives us peace in a time when there is no peace. God cares for them, (the Jews) He protects them, and He protects us.

You have to know for yourself that you are safe in Him; that is your heritage.

God created these people and gave them the ability to make the weapons that they were making, but then He lets them know it is not by Him that they gather.

Well, if God does not have them gathering who is it? It is the enemy, the devil.

God said they will fall and the reason they will fall is because of the Jews themselves.

That goes for you and I also; people fall every day because they come against the children of God.

We are no longer carnal, but spiritual; therefore you need to learn how to live in the Spirit and not in the flesh.

We are a powerful people because we have Jesus. Jesus said they would have no reason to fear, and neither do you.

I know that Jesus is watching you, and I am forever grateful.

Jesus lets them know that no matter what the people do in their planning and plotting, that they will never be able to use the weapons against them.

Jesus even gave them power against the judging tongue; He has given it to us also, so don't let what people are saying about you, or against you, get you down.

Christians spend too much time worrying about things they have no control over.

If you have been sitting up going through and afraid of your enemy, get up; and get moving in the name of Jesus, He has got you covered, He is your protector, thank Him now. Jesus also mentioned the fact that He is the one who will teach your children, so what are you waiting on? If you do not have your children in the house of the Lord get them there, they need Jesus in their lives more than ever.

If you are going to make it here on earth, in these trying times, you must be in submission to the Lord and His holy will. Submission will lead to genuine joy.

## Saul Lost It
(I Samuel 15:2-3)

Nothing left

Saul was commanded by Samuel to lead a holy war against the Amalekites; in other words, they were to destroy them, not some things but everything.

You have to be very careful when God speaks to you concerning anything. The one thing you need to do is be obedient, whatever He says to do, do it.

Saul spared the King, bought him back, and put him on public display, and he did this for his own glory. Greed will get you in big trouble, Saul looked at the cattle how fat and healthy they were and he bought them back too.

This was his plan all along (verse 12) he builds a monument to himself. Don't be tempted by what others have, we look from afar and wish we had what they have.

It does not matter what it is; I watch men today, God is calling them one way, and they want to go another. Why? Because they desire what others have, they are looking with the natural eye, instead of the spiritual eye; it makes no sense to do this.

You are just operating outside of your gift, and it won't work. God has called you to be a deacon, but you want to be a preacher, someone is blessed with a big house, as we say, so you want to go and get a bigger one. That is just crazy, because you can't afford what you have. Can you not see that this is a trick of the enemy? He wants to destroy you and your relationship with the Lord. When you do these kinds of things, you are saying to God, I know better than you, what is best for me.

Haven't you been attacked enough from the rear?

Saul tried to justify his deeds by saying he bought these things back as a sacrifice to the Lord; and that the soldiers insisted on his doing so.

You can't fool everybody especially those that have an intimate relationship with the Lord; and Samuel certainly had that. He came back on Saul and told him to obey is better than sacrifice, and to heed is better than the fat of rams. In addition to disobeying, Saul was guilty of rebellion, arrogance, and rejecting God's word. There are Christians today who fit this same bill, going out and doing things without God's permission.

Therefore what you are doing is lying on Him to justify your own actions. It's not too late for you because we serve a forgiving God; He loves you, and wants the best for you, (Verse 22). God is both faithful and compassionate; and He will restore His people to their special relationship with Him.

The worst scenario for Saul, is that he lost his Kingship (verse 26), you see when you reject God it is not a good thing. God turned away from Saul as King of Israel. When you lose with the Lord you have really lost. Even though the people recognized him as King for another fifteen years, God did not. He dropped him right then and there, (1 Samuel 16:14). The price you pay for your disobedience will be great. When God takes His Spirit away, He may just send you another spirit the same as He did Saul, an evil spirit. Now, can you see, you cannot blame the devil for everything; God is still in charge?

## Thanksgiving

(St. Luke 17:11-16)

He's Worthy

There is a shortage on giving God thanks for all that He has done. We should always take time to tell the Lord thank you. In the lesson scripture there is a bad case of bad manners. They were in a bad position and it was getting worse. Leper's had to always live on the edge; they could not be around anyone except other lepers.

If they attempted to do otherwise they would be killed. We have all got some things that we cannot share with others; and there are even some things we would not even dare put on a prayer list.

There are some things that are going to go with us to the grave, okay.

These lepers also had to cry out, when they came around, unclean, unclean.

They were somewhat isolated by their problem, problems do have a way of doing that too you.

Jesus was not in Jerusalem; He was between Samaria and Galilee.

He was walking through that place where they were struggling with right and wrong. Have you heard Galilee and Samaria talking to you lately? Paul said: every time I go to do right, evil is present.

Does it look as though while you were going through that Jesus was far away?

You know that feeling you get when He is far removed, I' am sure that you do.

## Scattered Thoughts

We have situations that can't be put on hold; we need to do as the lepers did, and cry out, Jesus hears us when we cry out to Him.

If you would just be humble, then the Lord will do the rest; just say, Lord have mercy, because mercy knows what you need; He is a loving Lord, and He will deliver you right on time, and when He does, don't you change on Him, you know, like some have done, and are still doing, they go home, sit down, and He never sees them again.

## Still Standing

(Zechariah 3:1-3)

Thank you, Lord

Satan had no power over Joshua, he was there at the angel's right hand, accusing Joshua of many things, (verse 2) and the Lord said to Satan, I reject your accusations against Joshua; Yes, I, the Lord, rebuke you Satan.

Joshua said nothing; he just stood in the presence of the Lord; that is all you have to do when the Lord is speaking.

He described Joshua as like a burning stick that has been snatched from a fire.

When you get hooked up with God the right way, you can be in the fire and not be burned, people may try and kill you and can't.

It gave Peter so much confidence that he even walked on the water.

We can pray and the whole house comes together, that's faith, (1 John 4:4) tells us greater is He "Holy Ghost" within us than he that is in the World (the devil).

If He had just been a mere man it would have been different. This is not the Joshua who walked with Moses.

Standing for me is enough to shout about because I am leaning on Jesus, therefore I cannot fall.

Joshua went to the Lord's house and stood up, you should do the same, and after all it was the Lord who bought you out, somebody needs to see your praise.

How well I know that He will do it, because He did it for me.

He has scars and messed up clothes; if you have got a scar and you can talk about it you surely ought to praise, because you could have been dead and gone.

The scar is your reminder that you are still here.

I praise God because He snatched me out of my mess before Satan could kill me.

I thank God that He has saved and sanctified me.

Jesus let Satan know that He chose Joshua; and He told him to let Joshua alone.

Satan is trying to point out to God how dirty you are; but, God is not having it because He has cleaned you up, you are no longer dirty, dirt, now you are clean dirt, sometimes spectators can mess up your worship; there were folks there looking at Joshua, and there are people looking at you too, no one knows what the Lord has done for you, therefore, they will never understand your praise, but I thank God, that the Lord surely does, to Him belongs all the praise, glory, and honor, Amen.

## Friday The Thirteenth

(Psalms 118:24)

This is the day that the Lord hath made; we will rejoice and be glad in it.

I have been moved by the Holy Spirit to write this particular Word today. Amazingly today is just that Friday the thirteenth.

If you are a Christian and I believe that you are, there are some things that you have got to let go of, being a Christian you have no business getting caught up in superstitions. Don't say that you haven't because He knows all things, just get it together.

You really do need to read and study the Word of God, because, when you get into His Word, then it is going to get into you.

Yes, we have all been there, (superstitious), and the truth be told, He is still delivering some.

*Here are just a few things to check yourself by:* For instance if you are driving your car and a black cat goes across in front of you to the left, and you turn around and go the other way, then you are superstitious,

If someone breaks a mirror in your home, and the first thing you say or think is seven years of bad luck, then you are superstitious, if you have a man come to your house on New Year's day to bring you good luck, then you are superstitious.

If a woman happens to enter your house on New Year's day before a man and you put her out, and sprinkle salt over one of your shoulders, then you are superstitious.

Okay, enough, I believe that you've got it. You need to know that every day that the Lord allows you to live is a day of thanksgiving, and I pray that after today you will never look at Friday the thirteenth the same way ever again.

Because when you look at who made it, you just know, that rejoicing is in order.

The Psalmist said: we will rejoice, who are we? We are those whom He has chosen as His own, we belong to Him we are God's property.

Jesus was sacrificed for us on the cross at Calvary.

Not only will we rejoice, but we will also be glad in it, I don't need anything else to convince me that Jesus is worthy, what about you?

The Lord has been rejected too many times, and it is always for many crazy and stupid things; want you turn back to Him today, pray His forgiveness, and live the rest of your life pleasing in His sight.

# My Blessings Are Chasing Me

(Deuteronomy 28:2)

God's Holy Covenant

When you have fellowship with God things will happen for you, God finds favor with His Children when they are obedient to His will.

One thing that we need to do as Christians is learn how to have an intimate relationship with Him, He is our Father and He deserves our time.

God gave us His all; He gave us His only begotten Son, Jesus Christ.

You need to imagine living your life according to His will and way, and do it.

Think of the times that He has both opened and closed doors just for you.

You have got to know that blessings do follow obedience, and that every choice has its consequences.

When you follow God you are blessed; when you do not follow God your life is cursed. The covenant was given to Israel that they might enjoy fellowship with God, and be prepared to receive His blessings.

There is a stipulation in this lesson: He says, which means something is connected here. (Verse 1) And it shall come to pass, if thou shall hearken diligently unto the voice of Jehovah thy God, to observe to do all his commandments which I command thee this day, that Jehovah thy God will set thee on high above all the nations of the earth. Read (Chapter 27:16-26) then you will see what the consequences are.

We have to make sure that our focus is on God and His Word.

I believe that after reading these verses you will begin to see a lot of things in life differently.

One of the main things that the Lord wants us to have toward one another is, love and respect, if you haven't been doing that, then maybe you have not stepped into the area of blessings.

It is not too late; it is imperative that we learn to do what we are told to do.

You should listen to God, because when you listen, then you will hear what He is saying to you; and then, you will receive your blessings.

## Hold On

(Matthew 9:20)

Not as easy as it sounds

Letting go is sometimes harder to do than one could even imagine, there is a great need sometime in our lives to let go of some things, or even someone.

But even in our letting go, there are some things that we need to hold on to.

You do need to let go of the hurt, but you need to hold on to the healer.

We all have to let go of something!

I' am sure that as you are reading this that something has surfaced in your mind.

You do know that holding on to things that we have no control over is a sin?

We have all got issues, some of which come, and some of which have gone, but some even have the nerve to move in with you.

The woman with the issue of blood had an issue with her problem; your problems can last for years, as did hers.

As I write this I think of even me Lord.

We have to learn how to turn everything over to Jesus; He is the only one that can handle what we are dealing with, and what we may go through.

There is something else, before she got better, she got worse. What about you? The truth be told; some of us, are in the same boat.

There is one thing that gives me the courage to go on; The Word of God, it assures me that it is always darkest before the dawn, (Psalms 30:5).

You may be at the door of your deliverance right now, so hold on, press on, and don't give up.

There is help for your issue, but you must believe it to be so, and then, you can, and will, receive your help.

Don't get discouraged as you wait, just wait patiently.

You must also admit that you have a problem, okay! Sometime the problem just may be you, oh yes, it's true, don't even act as though you are shocked at that statement.

How do you know that you may be the problem? Glad you ask; you know because the condition is on the inside of you, what is on your mind most of the time? Is it the work of the Lord? Is it going to the house of the Lord, and doing what you can to help make the world a better place? Or is it something that should not be there at all?

Well, there you have it, The Holy Ghost has gifted you, and it was not to sit around and do nothing.

What He has put inside of you is to be used according to His will. He deserves our very best, it is not about how you feel, or what you want to do, it is about soul saving, and pleasing the one who gave you eternal life, He is Jesus Christ our Lord.

## Don't Let The Devil Get In You

(St. Mark 5:1-5; 8; 12.)

Trust Jesus

Satan likes getting into the bodies of people, but there is still hope for all who will believe in Jesus.

This man had unclean spirits on the inside, and he had made his home in the tombs among the dead.

You can be brain dead, and you can be spiritually and morally dead.

This man was what we call crazy; he had no dignity, no decency, and no morals.

He allowed the devil to get inside of him, and when he does, he does not allow you to have any authority.

These are the signs of when he has taken you over: You use to enjoy going to Church, Sunday school, Bible class, visiting the sick, the prisons, and etc. Now you find excuses to keep from coming, and it does not bother you in the least when you miss, and when you do come, all you do is complain about the services, the ushers are not ushering right, the choir is not singing right, the pastor is not preaching good enough, the music is too loud, and on and on.

That is why sometimes we have to deal with a person's mind; Jesus did it, and as Christian we have to do it too.

Jesus touched the man, and healed his mind; the man ran to Jesus and worshipped Him. You must know who Jesus is, and you must worship Him.

Even the demons know Jesus; their response to Him was what do we have to do with you? Which is a very good and valid question, when Jesus encounters you, whatever is inside of you is going to come forth.

The demon spoke, and what was Jesus' response? Come out of the man, thou unclean spirit.

What is Jesus saying today? He is saying I want to deliver you.

Their response to Jesus was to let them enter into the swine, good Lord, even the swine did not want to be possessed by these demons; they went down the steep place into the sea and drowned.

Don't allow the devil to lead you, like some are so willingly doing, but let the Lord have His way in your life.

I would definitely rather have Christ in my life, than to deal with the devil and his foul evil ways.

When you let Jesus in, there is no place for the devil, now go out, and tell someone else the "Good News" about what the Lord has done in your life, He's just too great to be kept on the inside of you.

# The Power Of Giving

(St. Luke 6:38)

It is so real

If this subject has already caused your spirit to quench, oh well, you are in the right place. Debt does not get tired; debt is a money issue...

Some people just cannot figure it out, but, the more jobs you get, the less money you will have, in other words the broker you will get.

If you are not giving according to the Word you are living in bondage, debt is a destroyer it has destroyed many marriages, in fact it is what put most marriages in jeopardy, that four-letter word debt.

It is the one thing that most people get in trouble because of, debt.

We must learn to do things God's way, because it really is His way or no way at all, I' am sure you are agreeing with me so far.

The majority of people are getting paid, and not having enough money to do the things that they need to do, and, your money is already spent before you even get it, you are trying to live from pay check to pay check, and it's not going to work, because this is not God's way.

If you are ready, and you should be, God will bring about a change, but only if you let Him. Tithing is a place where everybody can change, but it is solely up too you. Don't get stuck on the tithe; that is your starting place. Every time that God said tithe, He also said pay, pay what? Pay your offering.

He also said give, the tithe is sacred and it is holy.

God said when we obey these things; He would, pour you out, more, than you have room enough to receive.

To give away, is the overflow. Tithing is an act of ownership and obedience it belongs to God... We must have faith and believe (Hebrews 11:6), without faith it is impossible to please God. You believe that He can wake you up, yet you want trust Him in the tithe and offering. You have to get past this robbing God.

You can be released from bondage, if you give, because giving is a heart issue; God wants you to understand the power in giving.

Everything that He made gives; let's see, the sun gives it light and warmth, the moon gives light to the night, the trees give fruit and shade, the earth provides a place for man and many other things, the sea roars in praise and provides a way of travel for man, the clouds give us shade and rain; now what does man do? Whatever you put in, that is what you are going get out, if you give little, then you will in return receive little, and if you give a lot, then you will in return receive the same. You need not think that you are deceiving God, because, you are not, He knows everything, (Galatians 6:7).

Sowing is a wise thing to do, and you always get more than what you sow, sowing implies very much to your getting out of debt.

Everything on earth started with a seed and multiplied, for example: the trees, no matter what kind they were, they multiplied; it is in the seed, God did not add any more trees.

This same thing applies today. It is time to cease being a spiritual felon, do as God has commanded; and He will do the rest, because our God keeps His promises.

## Use It Or Lose It

(St. Matthew 25:14-30)

One or the other

If you stop using your limbs for so long they will eventually stop working, you lose the ability to use them simply because you stopped.

That is what has happened to some of our spiritual gifts, they are not being used. There is even a saying, you use it or you lose it.

In verse fourteen they did not call Jesus He called them, Jesus has left us with His goods, and there is a grave danger when we say it is no big deal. The church is paralyzed, and it is that way because people are still sitting on their goods.

Many Christians do not use their gift, or gifts, because they think that they belong to them; wrong answer; you do have a gift, you must recognize it, and use it for the benefit of Kingdom building.

They recognized their gift, and responded to the opportunity to use them, they recognized their obligations. When you share your gift, it does not take away, it only adds more too you.

Jesus great gift, He took our sins, and gave us life, Praise God; that really obligates me to use what God has given me.

Nothing belongs to us, it is ours only by stewardship, and the gift is not yours outright it belongs to the Lord.

They traveled with it, they were trustworthy, and they were rewarded. Some of our gifts come from others indirectly.

They after a long time were still multiplying their gifts, because they used them.

In verse twenty-four he is justifying his shortcomings, the one that never moved, called Jesus hard.

Half of the truth is a whole lie. The significance of the gift, he was afraid, some Christians do not understand the gift giver. Not using your gift is to imply who is really over your life.

The reward is based on what you use, in verse twenty-one, Christ says, well done, my good and faithful servant. He also lets us know that to whom much is given, much is required.

We are gifted based on our own personal ability, Verse nineteen states, that after a long time, He came back; Jesus is coming back. So don't let Him catch you with His works, not yours, undone, because that, Christian friend is a trick of the enemy, the devil.

# When You've Had Enough
(1 Kings 19:4)

Turn it over to Jesus

Sometimes we as Christians get frustrated, because doing right is not what we want to do; there are days you just do not want to be bothered.

My pastor, would quickly tell you, that is spiritual burnout; he would also tell you that spiritual burnout will not leave on it's on.

Elijah was always needed by somebody for something, well; it is the same with some Christians, so don't you even start thinking that you are the only one; because I myself, can be a witness to that, you certainly are not.

God does not want to retire you, what God does is re-commissions us, if you have not recommitted, today would be a good day.

No one is ever too old to do the work of the Lord, even though there are some who think they are.

Be very careful when spiritual burnout sets in, a word of caution; do not go back to the wilderness, that is a dangerous move, don't you even dare play this way, sometimes it is best to just be still, don't go back to the things that you have been delivered from.

Just go in the presence of the Lord, like Elijah did, God can and will help you.

Learn how to call His name; He's patiently waiting on you. He is the one who will tear your mountain up; nothing is too big for our God.

Learn to listen for His still small voice, which is calling out to you.

The Lord told him to go, He is speaking to you now; can you hear Him?

He wants to use you, to help get others to where they need to be.

Know that when your faith becomes weak, and it will from time to time somebody else will be there to help pull you through.

Can anybody copy you, and get where they need to be in today's world? Only you possess the answer.

No matter how hard life gets for you; keep speaking positive, because all of our destinies have already been fixed.

God will move you, from brook ministry, to bread ministry, just keep calling on His holy name, He does hear you, and soon He will answer.

## Lessons From The Cross

(St. Matthew 27:35-36)

Having the characteristics of Christ

Our goal should be to live our life with the characteristics of Christ, I should always want to show more of Jesus and less of me, I should live like Him, Walk like Him, talk like Him, Love like Him, give like Him, and have a cross like Him.

The major problem is that many of us are trying to get the crowns of life, without the cross; without the cross, there is no crown. What comes after bearing the crown? Christ never mentions His cross without His burial and resurrection being mentioned.

If you are going to bear it, you have got to let God get you ready; He tells us in His Word, my yoke is easy, and my burdens are light, (that means well fitting).

What God is trying to get you to see is that He is wise enough, and that He is Omnipotent enough, to bless all mankind?

So stop complaining about your cross, whatever it is that has come against you, learn to say hallelujah anyhow.

There are those who are going through way greater things than you, and they are bearing it well. Many Christians are majoring on minor; your crowd needs to know what to look for from you, Jesus worldly enemies were present most of the time, when you are down the people who are around will treat you worse.

His religious enemies were there, it sure looks like His disciples would have been there also, but, that is just how it is, the folks that you expect to be there, are the ones that are not. Sin makes you blind; sin works from the inside out, the wages of sin is death.

It looks like a lot of other people would have been there because of all of the good things Jesus had done for them, but they were not.

What made the cross? God's ways are straight up; man's ways are sideways, God had healing; we had hatred, people need to know, that the cross was not pretty, like we made it to be.

When they checked them, to see if they were dead, they skipped the man in the middle (Jesus), God has a way of taking care of us, this did not happen by chance, Christ was in the middle for a reason; Christ's purpose is, to go between God, and man.

Jesus said, "If" I be lifted up, oh my Father in heaven, thank you! Look at who is between earth and heaven, oh it is Jesus, He did it for you and for me.

You have to know by now, that some things in your life; are just your cross. Christ enemies were enjoying His suffering, and so do yours.

Your enemies are real interested in what happens, when you are failing, or in trouble.

We have been bought out; Christ went through on that cross for something that He did not do, God has forgiven us, He has completed us, He has shown the critics, the curious, and the criminals, that He is all power; and because of Him we have the power to do whatever it is, that He would have us to do, and to do it with much greatness

## Now I See

(St. Matthew 20:30-34)

See What?

There is a blindness, which is worse than physical blindness; it is spiritual blindness. A lot of Christians deal with this on a day-to-day basis. It is true that you can be physically blind and go to heaven; and you can be spiritually blind and go to hell.

They could not see, so, they cried out; they made a lot of noise.

We can do some foolish things, and go to some foolish places, all because we were blind.

Well, you may as well know that some still are; they just refuse to give up the mess and join the winning team.

There is nothing greater, than serving, and praising the Lord God Almighty. And when you look back on your past, if you are really out; the only thing that you should be saying is, I positively and without a doubt had to be blind. Some people have joined church and are still blind, real truth.

There is a remedy for everything we cannot see, we have a Master who can touch us, and He brings sight to dark situations, and to our dark spots; (verse 30) when they heard, they responded, it was not because of what they heard, but it was because somebody made noise about Jesus.

In (verse 29) those who followed kept up enough noise for them to hear, you ought to keep up enough noise so that others will know where Jesus is. They should be able to hear you on your job, in your home, in your church, and anywhere else you go.

If you keep talking about Jesus, they will join you, it is very hard to hear the Lord's name and not get excited, I' am certainly a witness to that!

They accepted the Lord, a lot of us want the blessing, and the healing, but don't want to praise Him.

Christian brothers and sisters what are you doing with Him?

They cried, Lord we accept you for who you are; you must accept Jesus Christ as Lord and Savior, because that is who He is.

They accepted Him for what He wanted; (verse 31) they said Lord have mercy on us, aren't you glad that mercy knows what you need? I' am.

Don't you dare start talking about your rights, because if you got what you deserved, hell would have been your eternal home? But, God gives more grace to us than we deserve; He does it because He loves us. They agreed in prayer; whoever was talking agreed for both of them, we need to always pray for our families, church, job, and even pray for the we, our, and us, stop praying for I, my, and me, and when you do this God will get the honor and the glory, every Christian ought to have an us prayer inside of them.

What was it, you are asking, that made Jesus stand still? They gave Him their undivided attention; this is what we, as Christians should do, now, who has yours?

# Faith Beyond The Facts

(Daniel 3:17)

Facts are not reliable

A faith that fizzles before the finish is a faith not worth having.

What in the world did the young men do to find themselves standing on death row? They stood up! If you don't stand for something, you will surely fall for anything.

You don't have to fuss and make a show, if you have faith; it will stand up, and stand out; all on its own.

In this scripture the odds were against them; they were certainly going to be thrown into the fire. Fire is hot, and will consume you quickly; it will also kill you, now that is a fact.

People can cause pain in your heart, and you can't depend on them. A person can be your best friend today and be your enemy tomorrow.

When you stand for God, everybody else is not excited about it, people get mad at you, and they will not do anything with you, or for you.

In God's house, they stop participating in every thing; some even go home and sit down.

Some people don't like you because their friends don't like you; and what gets me is, that they do not even know you.

Others persuade too many Christians, when they are supposed to be following the Lord Jesus Christ.

They let these religious followers get them out on a limb, and can't get back under their own power; there is no way that they will make it, without the Lord.

What are you running and telling, just to get someone in trouble, or just to cause problems? (Verse 8) They ran back to the King and told it. (Verse 9) they made him feel good. (Verse 10) they reminded him of his law. (Verse 11) the consequences of his law? (Verse 12) they told him of certain Jews.

But, these men did not allow the new names to change their character; it is certainly not the name that makes you? I would rather a person know that I am a child of the King (Jesus) than to be going on about a name, (position). There is none greater than He.

They kept on standing, and they did not allow this to keep them from praying, because God was their comfort zone.

The same God that has allowed you to be where you are; is the same God that can bring you back down, so don't let your position, or your money; mess you up.

He gave them their positions; it is just a place where you can tell somebody about Jesus, there is someone out there waiting to hear, but they will not, until you deliver Him to them. Satan will always give you an alternative route; don't you take it! You can be sure that if you do, there will be some pain coming with it. You may even be pressured, but don't crack under the pressure and definitely do not apologize for doing what is right. We have a God of our very own, and as Christians we have got to be able to say who He is. He is my "I AM". You have got to know for yourself, that He is able to bring you through the fire, the flood, and anything else that you may find yourself in. I quote my Pastor in saying, "He's God, and He's got it like that", end of quote, trust Him always, He is present with you, even now.

# Life For A Dead Situation

(Mark 5:35-36)

Take off your grave clothes

You can't become deader, but you can decay more; there are some things in life that Jesus is not going to do for us, because He knows that we are capable, and wants us to do some things for ourselves.

Jesus is in the stone rolling business; He takes care of the weightier matters in our lives.

We are often times set free without even knowing it; it's time that we realized it and takes off our grave clothes.

When you take them off: put on, the whole armor of God, (Ephesians 6:10-18). Jarius comes to Jesus for help; we have the desire to come but don't.

You have to have the desire to do better, sad thing is, that a lot of Christians don't want to get better, they are satisfied where they are.

If you want something gone in your life then you will act like it, ask yourself this question, do you want it to get better? I pray that the answer is yes, but only you know.

You have to come to Jesus for yourself, and by yourself (v.22). Jesus needs to hear from you about your problem, instead of others coming to Him for you.

Have you ever earnestly taken your problem to God? If not, you need to establish a relationship with your Father, you need to know that you have your own connection with Jesus; he fell at His feet.

Have you ask the Lord to bless you according to His holy will? When you fall at the Lord's feet, you show humbleness to Him. It is a blessing to give reverence to the One who gave His all for you.

Be honest with the Lord when you pray, if you have been living a life of sin, say so, you can't fool God anyway.

Tell Him the truth, and be open about whatever it may entail.

He was concerned about his situation with God (v. 21), and he did not care who heard him praying.

He also came hoping, (v.23) he said, if you come, she is going to get better; you have to envision your situation getting better, then you have to act on what you believe, now that is faith. Some Christians allow Satan to keep them from seeing, but, faith say's see yourself getting better, or whatever the case maybe. God can, and He will, bring you through.

# Is God Worth Ten Cent?

(Malachi 3:7-12)

God has been good to us

God is a good God; He has kept us in the midst of danger; He has done so many good things for us and all He's asking for is one dime, out of every dollar.

My Lord! We truly are creatures of habit. I like doing, what I like doing, and if giving what I have is part of it, then I do not like it; sound familiar?

I have heard people make excuse after excuse as to why they should not give.

Well it doesn't matter what you think, if you are a Christian, and expect to be blessed, then you had better obey and give.

In verse seven God says return unto me and I will return unto you. Is this an indication that God is not present when I' am not doing what He has commanded me to do? I would say yes, it is so.

There was broken fellowship between the people and God, and it is still going on today. Broken fellowship leads to a broken relationship. He's telling us to come back to Him because we need Him.

When we repent godly sorrow it shows obedience. The Lord is my light and my salvation, and He is yours too, so trust Him to bless you when you obey.

A lot of people say tithing is not in the New Testament, well I beg to differ with you; it is certainly there, in (Matthew 23:23) Christ says these ought you have done; what? The tithe and offering.

The Old Testament is the foundation of the Word. We have got to get out of that Scribe and Pharisee righteousness. You do know that they were pious in their thinking, and were as wrong as you would be trying to wear two left shoes. Being an educated person does not make you a scholar of God's Word, (Matthew 5:20).

The Bible teaches us to study to show ourselves approved unto God, (2 Timothy 2:15).

I am not messed up about what a disbeliever has to say about the matter, when I say disbeliever I mean a religious person who has not yet reached their Christian status.

We are to stand on the Word of God. The tithe is holy (Leviticus 27:9). The tithe is a debt (Leviticus 27:31) when you don't pay; God has a way of getting it anyway.

God owes no one, but we owe everybody. (Leviticus 27:32) He said the tenth should be holy unto the Lord.

Now in verse eight He ask the question will a man rob God? Oh my! It is an awful thing to think about robbing God; yet it takes place every Sunday, and possibly, every day. You do know that in order to rob someone you have to be in his or her face, so what does that say to you? God said if we would give the tithe and the offering, He would hold back the destroyer Satan. When you don't do it you are only hurting yourself, God said it best, and you are cursed with a curse. Have you had any money troubles lately, family problems, sickness, etc? If so, it is all because you did not obey the Lord? But, in the end it never fails, you are the one who will pay.

*Scattered Thoughts*

# From A Member To A Worker

(Matthew 16:24)

What's your status?

If I were to ask you who you are, without telling me your name and where you work, whom would you tell me you are? You should be able to say more too me than things about your job. How much of you are made up by your Christianity? It is certainly very difficult to know everything in life. God has victory designed for those who will follow Him.

The church is full of members; our goal is not to see how many members we can get; but how many disciples we can make.

God is not looking for members. The church has too many members that just come and go to service, what's a couple of hours? That is no sacrifice. A member never considers going to Sunday school, Bible class, prison ministry, etc. Some of their excuses are: I can't do these things because they interfere with my favorite show, or I have to get my rest.

Have ever thought about what Jesus has done for you, how He gave His life willingly, and how He died for you, and much, much, more.

Being a disciple is much more than just being in a church and joining church.

Some members still have the same traits that they had over twenty years ago; there is no visible, or spiritual change at all. They don't like the other members; they still use profanity, and they are still committing adultery, and fornication. I could continue, but I believe you've got it. Please brothers and sisters, from one Christian to another, do not be satisfied with membership. Get yourself into a blessed house, where they are teaching and preaching the Word of God, and where they are involved in helping the surrounding community. This is what is pleasing in the Lord's sight.

You must be taught the ways of our Lord; this is why you must get in a good church where you can grow according to His plan for your life, He wants to develop you, and when you began to follow that plan, you began your walk in discipleship.

You be very sure that it is Jesus you are following; Peter said, Lord, if it is you then tell me to come to you, (Matthew 14:28). There are a whole lot of folk who know how to make them look right, when they are totally wrong.

The main thing that we should do is learning from the Lord, and do what He does; He is our role model. Peter saw Jesus walking on the water, and he did it too, (Matthew 14:25). There are a lot of things that look impossible, but they are not, when you follow the Lord Jesus Christ. What made Peter sink was a messed up focus; he took his eyes off of the Lord. If you are going to be a good disciple, Jesus is saying to you, now, it is time to get out of the boat. If you are a disciple and want to get better sanctify your environment, you cannot hang with everybody and be a good disciple, because hanging with the wrong folk will rub off on you; that is a fact. Discipleship is not necessarily getting what you need but exercising what you have. When you become a disciple of Christ, you become a blessing; and in return, you will receive blessings.

# No One Is Good Enough To Go To Heaven

(Psalms 139:17-24)

You need Christ

Listen, you need Jesus! We can easily denounce the drug addict, the prostitute, and all those that we consider to be the sinful people of the world.

What about you dear friend, what are you doing from day to day?

As a Christian you should be busy doing the work of the Lord; instead of being a busy body, a gossip, and The Lord only knows what else.

But the fore mentioned are the standards we have set for our own selves.

We say we are doing nothing wrong, but do you really believe that?

If you do you are really setting yourself up for a great ride.

We only see the other person's sin, I have often wondered, why are we not as strict, or hard, on ourselves as we are on others.

You see what you do as nothing and okay, you are always right, and you make no mistakes, yeah right.

After praying that God would judge his enemies, the Psalmist turned the spotlight on him, (v. 23). He said, search me, O God, and know my heart, try me, and know my anxieties; and see if there is any wicked way in me. How interesting it is that he would speak this, when he already knew that it was. But still he asks God to check him out; and then he asks that God would lead him in the way everlasting.

He has shown us that we need to go to God about our own selves, because He is the only one who will, and can correct us. And when God does, it cuts to the very marrow in our bones, (that's deep).

I thank God for the Psalmist, because he lets us know that it does not matter how saved you are, you still need Jesus to lead you and guide you. If heaven is to be your home, you must depend on Him (Vv. 23 – 24) he lets us know it is not wrong to stand against sin wherever it occurs no matter who it is, even if it is within you.

There is something else here that you need to take too heart; it is a tragic mockery of God's grace to judge others harshly while you are being lenient on yourself. If you have done this or are still doing it, pray. If you are a victim still pray, God knows and He is the soul judge. It is time that we learn to treat everyone with the love of Jesus, not just those whom you choose to love and care about. After all, this is what "The Savior" is about, showing love to everyone, try it, as a Christian you will learn to love it.

# A Good Example To Follow

(Job 1:1-8)

Only One Righteous Man

How can you be a critic of someone when you don't really know what he or she are going through or dealing with? It certainly is not an easy thing to lose someone to death, or to lose something period, and even if you have, you still don't know what the other person is feeling. Although this saying has been used for years and years, I do know what you are going through; I beg to differ, you do not.

Job really went through some things, and he suffered a lot, it was one catastrophe after another. I do wonder if we would be able to stand a test like that!

I truly do believe that you can survive anything if you have the Lord to see you through it. Job lost all of his children, and his wife was crazy, she told him to cuss God and die; and his friends; they were no comfort at all.

The Word of God tells us that Job lost everything that he had, and yet he never turned his back on his God, that is amazing.

Would you be able to endure what came after, as well as the before?

Job feared God and he respected Him. The Lord knows whom He can, and cannot depend on. Can you truthfully say that you totally depend on God? Be honest with you. Are you devoted totally to Him?

A lot of Christians are only devoted as long as things are going their way.

What would happen with you, if God stopped showing love, and meeting your needs? Would you perish, or would you survive? Would you be a spiritual mess; like the sheep that have lost their Shepherd?

You know sheep only see what is right in front of them because they have tunnel vision.

Job loved his family; and he had a good relationship with his friends.

The Lord God is looking for men and women who are devout; men and women who will obey His will and His Word.

Sometimes things in life will happen quick and sudden, and it seems as though you are not even able to breathe, all because of how fast it comes.

Trouble does not discriminate; it visits everyone, and every family.

There is only one real option for us all, His name is Jesus Christ.

He will, and He can bring you through, whatever it is that comes your way.

He will be your strength in the time of your storm, why not trust Him to the end of your journey. God does allow things in our lives on a daily basis. I found out in my going through that it really does make you stronger that are what our trials come to do; they come to make you strong.

# Don't Go Home The Same Way You Came

(Luke 13:10-12)

Get what you need

There is more to church than just coming and going, when you enter the house of the Lord you should be expecting to receive a blessing, I sure do!

Not only do I expect it; I do get what I came for. As my Pastor would say, if you come with what you always come with and receive nothing; then you will leave the same way that you came. You have got to raise your expectation. That to me is so imperative, that something happens to lift and encourage me when I enter the house of the Lord.

What made her go home better? The truth is we have become professional churchgoers. Going to the house of the Lord will make you stronger, because the Word of God will build you, in mind, body, soul, and spirit.

A lot of Christians do not want to be taught sound doctrine but that is the main thing that is going to help you grow. You cannot go around in ignorance the rest of your life; you should want to know what it is that the Father has for you.

You should also want to learn so that you will one day be able to teach someone else, if Jesus thought it was right to teach, so should you.

When a Christian does not eat the Word of God, he or she becomes weak because of the rejection.

Jesus was teaching on the Sabbath, (v.11) she was in attendance, she was sick, but she still came to church. When you learn better, you should do better.

Even with all your problems you need to pull yourself up and get back in the house of the Lord.

The Psalmist said I looked at the prosperity of the wicked and my foot almost slipped. The woman was crooked and bent over from her infirmity. It makes no difference whether you are bent over or standing straight up, if you are soul sick, the only cure for that is; the Word of God. (v.16) Satan had her bound; she could only look down,

That is where a lot of Christians are today; they are looking down on everyone and everything. You have also got to stop looking at the symptom, and home in on the source, your central focus as a Christian should be on Jesus Christ and no one else. He is the reason you are here, He is the reason you are saved, and He is the reason you are on your way to heaven. The Lord uses the Angel of the church (your Pastor), to give you what you need, every time you enter the house, (the church). It comes from the pages of His holy Word, the Bible.

Through him (the Pastor), Jesus reveals to us what we are supposed to have, in order to make it through, no matter what it is that you may be going through.

Every Sunday, Wednesday, or whatever day you are in attendance; all over the nation and world, God's Will is being read. The question is, are you present for the reading? Can you hear what he is saying too you today? The answer is also in this Word; and it is this, Man, Woman, Boy, and Girl, you have been loosed.

## Keep Hope Alive

(1 Peter 1:3-6 13)

Hope in the Lord!

This is a great quote from the Rev. Jesse Jackson. But how do we put it into our everyday life situations? Glad you ask; there is going to be times in your life when you will have good days, and there will be times when they will not be so good, in some you will be up, and in others you will be down.

We define that as happy or sad, feeling good or feeling bad, sun shining or cloudy with over cast skies, some even say they are having a blue Monday. But regardless of which one you may be in, or think you are in, I bring you Good News, and you can make it.

One of the ways a Christian keeps hope alive is by what is exalted (v.3) blessed is the God and Father of our Lord Jesus Christ. We should always talk good about others, but that is not the case; and you should know that God will never die, "Praise the Lord", for He has been raised from the dead, again, "Good News".

Some Christians cannot even talk about God because they do not really know Him, the only way to know the Father is to get into the Word.

If I am going to keep hope alive in my life, I have to know what to hope for. You can hear the testimonies of others, but you should have one of your very own.

God has surely blessed you in some way, the only way to keep hope alive is to bless God; this is where your hope lies.

He is an "Awesome God" His mercy is abundant; and it overflows to His children, God's mercy is new every day.

He is truly the God of more than enough, so no matter what comes your way; just know that God has got it.

It is the mercy of God that has brought us to live expectations. I expect great and wonderful things in my life because of Jesus Christ, what about you?

You can count on the Lord God at all times and in every situation, because He will always be there for you, He says I will never leave you, nor will I ever forsake you.

Your expectations can never outgrow His ability; and because of the resurrection, you can always count on the Lord Jesus Christ.

Why? Because He is our hope, and He keeps His Word, Jesus never fails, (v.13) holiness is commanded, and holiness is a lifestyle, it not something that you do on Sunday morning for two hours, and then the rest of the time do what you like. If you are His then you will obey, and live holy.

## God Sent Him
(1 Kings 17:9)

Respond in faith

The Holy Spirit is speaking, and what He is saying to us is that we are needed. There should be a willingness to go a little farther in the name of Jesus. How far are you willing to go? God does have a mission for each and every one of us. Elijah has been a very obedient servant of the Lord; He prayed, and God stopped the rain, now that my friend is power.

What is it that seems to make us weak in our doing? God fed him, he used a bird one that was normally a taker, and made him a giver.

Don't you know that if God can change the nature of a raven, He can, and certainly will do the same thing with you, change your nature?

God will let you go on and on, until you get tired. One day your brook is going to dry up; and when it does, you will have to move on. Elijah did not complain when he had to move, if Elijah had not moved on, then the woman and her son would not have been.

It is very good to be obedient; you just may be the one that He will send to stop that person from committing suicide, or shooting someone else, etc. I believe you have a visual now.

When God sends you, that which He sends you too, and to do; shall come to pass.

The main thing is you have to trust Him and keep yourself out of the way because self loves to get busy.

The woman's first yes to Elijah did not cost her anything; all he asks her for was a little water, (v.10). It was the second yes that was going to cost her.

The first yes for you, is Salvation. The second yes, is service, and they are both left up to you; most Christians stop at the first yes, because when you go further it requires something, it challenges you, and your life. You have to realize that it is no longer about what you want, but what He wants is all that matters.

Do you only work for the Lord when it fits your schedule, or do you do it even when it does not?

Challenging your commitment is going to cost you, you must have some standards about yourself. It does cost you when you want something in your life. "As the saying goes, nothing is free". If you want the Lord to bless you, you have to pay your part, are you willing to alter your plans, if God say's to; think about it, the woman would not have survived, had she not altered her plan, she and her son would have starved to death. You do know that was her initial plan, to die.

He teaches us how to trust Him. What are you and your church doing to better the community, the State, the Nation, and the World on a natural basis? He also teaches us how to reject fear, supernaturally, because fear is a trick of the enemy, (Satan). He always teaches us how to respond in faith, because obedience should always come first, why not trust your life to the Father today?

# Winning Over Worry

(Matthew 6:25-34)

Why not today?

Worry has no respect of persons; it causes many things to go wrong in the body.

Worry is a sin and if you are not careful Satan will slip it right in on you.

A lot of people are in a state of worry right now. You can't pay your bills, car note is past due, you owe the doctor, etc.

A lot of people are suffering with stomach ulcers, bad nerves, body aches, etc. But still you continue letting it take root within; everything hurts your feelings, you are moody, it is nothing but worry.

You can solve nothing by doing this, yet you do it anyway. You lose your joy, when you worry, to the devil. Know that if he gets your joy, he will take your strength.

It is most important that we know these things because Jesus moves from prayer to talk concerning worry. He cares for us, and He loves us so much.

As a Christian you have got to learn how to have a good prayer life! We may say we pray, but we do not petition the Lord as much as we should. I know that's right. The truth is the light and it will make you free.

If you were praying, and believing what you are praying for you would not have a lot of the problems that you have. (I don't know what you are going through but the Holy Ghost does). You must be sincere when you pray, and then you will get up positive and not negative. Why?

Because when you talk to the Father, you know that everything is going to be all right! There will be no sign of worry, and there will be no room for it either.

Worry has never made a problem go away, and it definitely is a tool of the enemy, (Satan), he uses it constantly against us.

Worry is not a good thing, because when you do it; you take away God's glory.

What statement are you making? When you worry you have become self-centered, and you have begun to doubt God.

He is the one who has given you everlasting life through His Son Jesus Christ, so ask His forgiveness, and move on.

If you really believe that the God we serve is Omnipotent, then why do you worry? Now, get back your joy, and your strength, in the name of Jesus.

# The Order Of Service

(Psalms 100:1-5)

Praise Him!

There is a certain way that you should do things in the house of the Lord!

God Himself tells us what He wants of us. He wants us to shout, and serve.

If you are a true worshipper then you will serve the Lord with gladness.

People seem to get everywhere they go on time except the house of the Lord; that is doing the Lord a disservice. Yet you feel it is okay; well it is not, and it is time for a change; Going to Sunday school and Bible class are important factors in the life of a Christian.

There is real joy in serving the Lord for a born again saint.

(Psalms 107) tells us to let the redeemed of the Lord say so; you should want someone to know that you are a child of the King.

If you really know who He is, then tell it to somebody; let them know what and who He is to your life.

Even the sinner knows Him, for we are all His creatures, but they only know Him as God their creator.

We who are saved and sanctified know Him as Our Lord and Savior.

If you really know Him then your purpose should be to give Him a naked praise, that is to say, leaving all the stuff out of it, and just praising Him for who He truly is.

He is God, He is Lord, He is Savior, and He is Holy Ghost. To me "He is "I AM THAT I AM". He is much, much, more, but that really says it for me.

He tells us we are His people, and that we are the sheep of His pasture; that's love. It means that He is our Shepherd and He is taking care of us daily.

David said it best, when He said, The Lord is my Shepherd and I shall not want; now that is personal.

You have to make Him personal in your life; you are the only one who can.

You can hear the preached Word Sunday after Sunday, but, it does you no justice; if you do not get Him into your heart where He belongs.

You need to praise Him daily; you need to Praise Him for your past, present, and for your future, for it is God who has bought you through. Praise you, the Lord.

# Who Has The Best View?

(Psalms 102:19)

Certainly it is you Lord

Yes it is so very true that God has the greatest view in the entire universe.

We can only see so far, but, He sees all, and He knows all.

The Word of God lets us know that heaven is His home, and that the earth is His footstool.

One day we will take our place with Him in that beautiful city called heaven.

A city not made by human hands; a city not tainted in any kind of way.

In that great and beautiful city we will have our own mansion, oh God, how awesome. Heaven, what a wonderful place; aren't you glad that the Lord God is All Power?

He looks down upon the earth from day to day, and He never sleeps.

So whatever it is that you are going through know that you are not alone, He is ever present.

When you lay down to sleep at night, He is looking down on you, He has given His heavenly angels charge over you and me; He is your protection, He keeps you from all hurt, harm, and danger.

Your soul should be pleased to know that you have a Father who cares.

There are a lot of Christians who are going through things unnecessarily, all you need to do is let Him have His way no matter what it is.

He's God, He can, and He will bring you through. I thank God for being on His heavenly throne, and for having the power to bless us forever more.

We do not have to beg for a blessing, the Word tells us to trust Him and depend on Him.

The very best place that any of us can ever be is in the arms of Almighty God.

I am so happy that He protects us, and loves us.

Nobody will ever love you like the Father does, you can rest assured in this because it is true.

 I myself have been through some terrible things in this life, but He has never failed to see me through. What about you? This brothers and sisters, is all the more reason that we should praise and glorify Him.

## Children Changed By A Touch

(Matthew 19:13-15)

Jesus can and He will

If Jesus did it we are to do the same; the trouble with our children today does not lie with the children, but it is with the parents.

Parents today are too lenient with their children. They reward them for doing nothing and I do mean nothing. They give them expensive gifts at Christmas time and some even more than that. Every time they enter a store with you they think that they should receive something; and you give it to them, this is very unhealthy for your child.

God is holding you responsible for the raising of your children. It is so amazing how parents of today pamper their children, and they get nothing in return for it. They talk to you any kind of way and you take it. Something is terribly wrong with this picture. Jesus gave the greatest example of how to raise your child. He laid hands on them; children need to be touched, and loved.

There are two ways to love a child you can love them to life, or you can love them to death, which one are you doing?

There is a consequence for doing it the wrong way! They will not know how to love if you never discipline them and let them know they cannot have everything that they want. It is not good for anyone to live like this.

Everyone needs to be disciplined, or you will go around thinking that the whole world owes you something.

The next thing that Jesus did was, He prayed for them to go together (touching and prayer). How can you not pray for your children? God has given you charge over them; but for some reason parents have gotten this real out of whack. You are to be a good Stewart over your children, and be the best parent that you possibly can.

The next thing is, that Jesus said suffer the little Children to come unto me, and forbid them not, are you taking them to the house of prayer? Well if not, do it! A lot of your problems would be solved if you would just follow the Will, (the Word of God). If you are holding them back from Him you are walking on some dangerous ground. You can change, get it together, get up and get them there.

He ended it by saying; it belongs to them, the Kingdom of heaven. That should be enough to awake anyone out of their terrible sleep. There is nothing wrong with doing what the Lord has told you to do concerning the raising of your children. The wrong is in you're not doing what He is telling you to do. If you want peace concerning the raising of your children, begin today being obedient to the Lord. After all it did not hurt you when your parents disciplined you. Christian parents, I pray you will take this to heart, for the Word of God is before you, concerning those that He loves, and secondly; that you love, your children. You cannot go wrong if you yield to the Will of the Lord. Jesus did what He came to do, and then He departed, He is doing the same thing today. He gives you the opportunity to be the best parents that you can be. Don't make Him sorry that He trusted you, and don't let Him down.

## It's Your Season

(Ecclesiastes 3:1)

Thank you, God

From the heart of one who loves the Lord with everything; I know that this is true. It is the season of plenty for those who love and obey the Lord. God is moving by His power in the vessels of those who will be obedient to His holy will.

Are you one of those vessels? If your answer is yes, then you are on your way. God has opened a door for the Christian that cannot be shut by any means. It is work time, it is praise time, it is hallelujah time, it is thank you Jesus time.

He is so worthy to be praised; not because He has opened a door of plenty for you, but because He is God; and He is Worthy to be praised. God said that we would be the head and not the tail, do you believe it? Whether you do or not doesn't matter, because God's Word does not, nor will it ever, fail.

God is not depending on you, but you sure had better be depending on Him, you need Him as much as you need the air He provides for you to breathe.

God has come, and is taking His children to another level those that have been prepared to go.

I am nervous as I write this because I feel the Holy Ghost moving in me. I wish that as a child of God I could help you to see it. But I cannot, the same way that He is touching me now, He can and will touch you.

There is a stipulation here, and the proper words would be, if you will let Him.

Christian men and women let Him have His way, He is your Father and He does have great things in store for you. Are you aware of the fact that someone is waiting to come to Christ right now; the sad thing is they cannot come until you get in place, because you are the one that they will come through?

You have a responsibility to your fellow man to get in place; stop holding up progress. Won't you let Him take you higher? It is time to let go of the things of the world, as the Scriptures in this chapter will speak to you.

What is it that you have to let go of before you can climb under the unction of the Holy Ghost If you are a Christian you can hear God calling you, so don't keep Him waiting any longer. If you are in the church get busy, if you are not get going. When you start too step, He will go right along with you; leading you all the way. God is Our Father who never fails.

# Let It Go

(Genesis 27:41; 33:4)

Turn it over to Jesus

What is it in your life that has altered who you are? What has happened in your life that you do not even want to talk about it? I am sure if you really think about it, you will come up with something or someone. It could have been something from your childhood, and for some, it could be your adult life. We have all had to deal with and go through some things, that we found not be favorable for us at all.

Some Christians are dealing with some of those things right now. You see people today who are living their lives the way they choose. They have poor self esteem, and they are depressed. They feel that no one loves them, including their own family. How sad it is that no one can reach them, or tell them anything, and yet, they are saying, that they know the Lord.

Well, it does not matter what you have experienced in this life, in your past, or in your present, God can handle it. There is no problem that is too big for your Father. Not only can He handle it; He wants you to relinquish it to Him, and see exactly what He can, and will do. So, why not, turn it over to Jesus. After all, you should be worn out by now from wrestling with it all of these years let it go! Your freedom depends on it. What will it take for you to turn it loose? Are you going to be an Esau? He had to deal with his major resentment toward his brother Jacob.

Sure we get angry when people hurt us, and abuse and misuse us; but, we cannot live that way, we have to keep on keeping on.

Resentment comes from the pain that we have to deal with. We see in the scripture where Isaac wept seriously, because of what Jacob had done to him. Be careful of what the pain can cause you to do and even say.

For example: we have a saying when someone gets on our nerves; she makes me sick or he does; you had better watch that, those are killing words that you have just spoken on your own body.

We begin to plan and plot on those who have hurt us, because we have gotten caught up in our thoughts about it. We quickly forget that vengeance belongs to the Lord, (Romans 12:19); revenge gets you nowhere; it is a trick of the enemy (Satan).

God's Word tells us to be not deceived for God is not mocked; whatever you sow, you will also reap, (Galatians 6:7). You can be right about someone, but, it is not your place to straighten them out. Once again, let it go, God will punish the one who gets in the way. Another way to look at this is; you become a prisoner to the problem, and the person is going on with their life, and most of the time you are not at all on their mind, and neither is what took place between the two of you. How do you know that you have resentment? Well, if someone mentions the person, and you relive it, if it makes your nerves crawl, or turns your stomach, that is resentment. There you have it. Paul said that we are to press on toward the mark of the high calling of Jesus Christ, so let Him have it, and let it go. Jesus is the Author and finisher of your faith; not man, trust Him.

## Being A Friend

(Proverbs 18:24)

Whose friend are you?

People come into our lives and they go out. But who is really a friend? Is it the person that you have attached yourself too? In order to have a friend you must first present yourself friendly.

A friend is one who will be there for you no matter what! It doesn't matter how far away a friend is, they will always be thinking of you, caring and praying for you.

All Christians have a true friend in Jesus Christ; He is a friend who is closer than any brother or sister.

We are blessed to have the Lord in our lives, with Him you are never alone; there are some who consider everybody that they meet a friend, this is far from the truth.

A friend will be closer too you than a brother or sister, this is the Word of God.

It's true in the world today; families say they love one another, but they are really not there for one another. When you need someone to talk to, the best person too call is a friend.

(Proverbs 17:17), The Lord God does not falter in His Word, man on the other hand falters all of the time. God knew what He was doing when He set the Word in place.

A brother and sister will be at odds with one another, but a friend will always be there for you. I believe that you love your family members, and so do I.

But, the truth be told, they are not as close to you as a friend. You see the truth is the light, and it will make you free.

Don't sit reading this with a stubborn spirit; let the Holy Ghost show you the real truth.

I thank God for my family, and I love them dearly, but I also thank Him for my friends.

Give God the glory, the honor, and the praise for who He really is to you.

In case you may be wondering who my number one friend is I have no problem letting you know, His name is Jesus.

He is a friend who sticks closer than any brother or sister, Jesus will go with you when you enter into the storm, He will stay with you while you are in the storm, and He will be at your side when it is time to come out of the storm. Simply said, He will go with you to the end.

In case you don't know Him, get to know Him, this would be a great day to give The Lord Jesus your life. I assure you, you will be glad that you did.

# Destined For Destruction

(Philippians 3:17-19)

Are you an enemy?

My walk should let others know who I am; in other words, the life I live should be speaking for me. Your walk is your life, how are you living today?

I pray it is for God and not for you; Paul encourages us to walk as he did, and to be an example. He lets us know that he was not perfect in his walk, and neither are we.

Your walk should be a great example to those who see you, each and every day. People should be able to look at you, and see, that there is truly something different in your life walk, than theirs.

They should be able to say, I want to get to where they are in their walk with the Lord. They should be able to come to you for guidance, can they?

Are you showing Christ-likeness in your Christian walk? You should not be living a life that is conflicting with who you are supposed to be, only you would know this for sure, and of course, the Lord Jesus.

Those who are presented in our Scriptures today were living a life that was pleasing to them, but not too God, that is a dangerous thing living the life of an anti-Christ.

As a believer, you should be able to determine the difference between truth and error. When people have real concern for the people around them, they will weep for them, simply because you want them to get to where God is trying to take them.

This is not a game that you and I are in, and you think that maybe one day you will wake up from it, this my friend is real life. This will determine your destiny; will it be heaven or will it be hell?

Listen at what he is saying about these people, as enemies of God they were destined for destruction, and the same applies to you, you will either be with Him, or you will be against Him.

So do the right thing, lives are depending on you, it is not good to put your trust in your own self, and you will fail every time.

Listen as these false teachers talk, does anything you are hearing sound familiar to you? If so turn it over too Jesus, and let Him bring you out.

He say's their god is their stomach, they had in mind only their own physical desires and thoughts, only of what they would eat. (Have you ever been there)?

Their glory is in their shame, instead of giving glory to God, they praised themselves, and had pride (not good at all), this pride consisted of things they should have been ashamed of, but they were not.

Their earthly desires outweighed their heavenly desires. You will not get anywhere like this with God; He cares about your earthly needs, but, His desire, is that we learn how to live spiritually, that is what pleases Him.

# He Is Our Amazing Grace (John 1:14)

Lord Jesus

The Word became flesh "Logos" Jesus Christ, who is God the Father, came to earth as a man, He did not just look like a man, He became a man for the benefit of mankind. He did not change, praise God, but He certainly changed us, He added us to Himself; those of us, who would become just like Him.

He took on a human nature, which means, He felt just like we feel; He could understand our hurt and pain, because as a human man, He knew exactly what we have to deal with on a daily basis.

Even as a man He was not exactly like us, because in His fleshly body He kept Himself unspotted from the world.

He did not come to stay in that form; He was needed to do a job that no other sacrifice, or man, could do.

We were in trouble, and God knew that something had to be done in order for us to get back to Him.

So Jesus, our Amazing Grace, said I'll go. You should be very grateful that He loved you so much that He was willing to give up His place in heaven for a period of time to come to earth and deal with people like you and I.

He came that we would be free of our sins, and to show us the way, for we certainly did not know the way.

We had been separated from Him by the sin of one man (Adam), but, Jesus changed it.

Now we are able to go to the throne of Grace for ourselves, we don't have to wait on anyone else too get through for us.

Some people of that day saw His glory; John was one of them, he was an eyewitness to what took place before we came on the scene.

I' am glad John saw the Lord and His glory; that glory is still working miracles today in the lives of His children.

This brings to mind that one day we will be able to do the same; we will see Him for ourselves. Our eyes shall behold His glory, the same as John did.

Only it will be greater, because we will be with Him, in heaven, never to worry, cry, and be in pain, sickness, sorrow, or suffering, ever again. His glory shall be the light of heaven.

What joy, there will be no more bills, and pesty little people on your telephone? Christ Jesus is God's Son; and He is very different than you and I. We were made to be His children, by the death of Jesus on the cross at Calvary. Jesus has been God's Son since the beginning of time. This is a gracious and truthful revelation to all who will believe. He was full of grace and truth, God said it, that's it, to Him is the glory, Amen.

# He Gets The Credit

(1 Corinthians 15:10)

A good worker

It is very true, that we are, who we are because of Grace. Grace works wonders in your life. God gives grace to us, it is a gift.

You have in no way done anything to deserve it, and you cannot do anything that will make you a rightful recipient of it.

Grace is God's unmerited favor, He looked at you, and decided that He wanted you to have it; it is not because of you, or anything that you did, but it is because of His darling son, Jesus Christ.

Are you grateful for this grace that is in your life? Paul said it best when he said, it is by the Grace of God that I am what I am; this is true. Paul was one of the greatest preacher/evangelist that ever walked the earth, and he was true to his calling. When the Lord Jesus changes you that is how it should be.

There is so much work to do; and by now, most of us should know what it is that we are supposed to be doing. Question is: are you doing it?

Grace is timeless, and it will follow you throughout eternity. Problem is, that time is not. Each of us has a time frame on our lives, and one day, the curtain is going to be drawn (death).

That is why we must work now, those things that He has given us to do. God's Word tells us that night is coming, and when it does, you will not be able to work anymore.

So, do all that you can now! Jesus gives us an opportunity to contribute to the building of the Kingdom of God, each and every day. Are you letting your opportunities pass you by? Paul was a great builder of churches, most of which he did from the walls of a prison.

You have that same opportunity, to help others come too Christ and be saved. But, what are you doing with what He has given you?

If you are getting things done in the name of Jesus, be aware of this fact, it is not you doing it; it is God, He does it through you, you are just the vessel that He has chosen to do it through. He created you to use as He wills.

If you are not doing what He desires of you to do, then it is time you got in position.

Remember, time is not eternal, but the Grace of God is; so stop saying what you cannot do, because you can do all things through Christ, (Ephesians 4:13) and by doing so, you will please your Father which is in heaven.

# The Trinity

(2 Corinthians 13:14)

The Father, Son, & Holy Ghost

It is good to receive a blessing from someone in authority. I am reminded of people who go to church hear the word and leave without receiving the benediction from the Pastor. What's the hurry? The restaurant is going to be there when you get there.

We need all of the blessings that we can get. In this world that we are living in it is most imperative that we get all that we can.

Paul is writing this salutation, he was staying with the saints of Macedonia, he is sending out a unified greeting to the saints at Corinth. It also speaks to man today, because the Word of God is for everyone that will accept it.

The believers at Corinth have finally become obedient to the Word of God, and they are now receiving a blessing.

Blessings come when we are obedient to God; and also when we are following whom He has placed to lead.

God is a God of order; there is no going out and doing things of our own power.

We have seen what happens when we do, and it is not a pretty picture.

So stay under the umbrella of your leader; and God will be your protection.

The Pastor invokes the same blessing on us at the benediction; this blessing comes from the Triune God.

The grace is given to us through Jesus Christ, and God the Father's love is expressed, (Agape).

The fellowship that we enjoy comes because of The Holy Ghost, if He is in you, you will have fellowship with one another, not just a select few, because in the eyes of the Father everybody is important.

That is why we are still here, because He wants as many as possible to be saved.

God knows what He is doing, and He does not need your help to do it, why not? Glad you ask, because doing it His way works, and He never fails?

Always show appreciation and honor to the one who has given you everlasting life, show Him how much you really love Him, and care; by doing what you should, to make sure that others receive this same love and salvation that you have already received.

## Joy Comes In The Morning
(Psalms 30:5)

Bless your name Lord

It is very crucial to have joy in your life; if you are a Christian you know that joy is a requirement and that we have control over our joy.

James tells us we are the captains of our joy. The Psalmist tells us that joy comes in the morning.

Well, why are a lot of Christians so without it? Simply because they do not believe that they have the power to overcome whatever it is that is bothering them.

But, the Word of God say's that you have the power to overcome.

It is hard to understand why so many Christians stay in depression, and close to depression; when all you have to do is trust, read, meditate, and believe in Him.

If you don't get this inside of you, it will never work. The Word of God has to get deep down inside of you.

The other obstacle you need to overcome is; that you have to let The Holy Spirit have His way in your life.

It is not healthy to keep Him locked down day after day, while your flesh rules. He has been trying to get your attention for a long, long time, let Him have it, it belongs to Him.

When you gave your life to Christ; it gave Him the right to send to you The Holy Ghost. He did not send Him that He would lie dormant in you, but that He would lead and guide you into all truth.

If you let Him, He will be your company, your friend, and your confidant. God has delivered you through His Son, and from this deliverance should come praise and worship.

Who else do you know that is worthy? I know no other, but the Lord Jesus Christ.

He has saved you from your sins; He has even saved you from yourself; that alone should give you joy.

Have you ever thought that somewhere along this journey that you may have angered God? Well, truth be told, we probably all have. So now you too can say as the Psalmist did, let us sing and praise Him, for truly; His joy is coming in the morning.

# A Good Day To Obey

(2 Corinthians 10:5)

Jesus is waiting

Every day you rise up out of your bed is a day to obey; it is a day to love on your Father, God.

Matter of fact it is the only day that you get to do it. God is so good to us, and so generous. Some have lived to see old age, and still do not choose to give Him the praise that He deserves.

Do you not know that this is what you were created to do? Praise Him.

Most people spend their time running and doing the things that are important to them. Do you not know that if it were not for the Lord, you would not be able to do anything? You would not be able to get up out of your bed.

But, because of Mercy, you got up this morning; that should be enough for you to realize that you need to thank and praise God. Have you ever given thought to all of the things that He has done for you, and for your loved ones?

You could not count them even if you tried; it is senseless to do so.

God is waiting on you today, to do that one thing that He has put in your spirit; only you know what that is. It may just be a kind word, or it may be treating someone else with the respect that you want to be treated with. Whatever it is, get it done.

As a Christian you have got to learn how not to be slothful; you must do what He wills in your lives, and for your life.

As I write this Word today, I am praying that God would be moving in the hearts of His people; I pray that you would be led by The Holy Spirit, and I pray that you would let Him have His perfect way in you. Why? Because what you have already done will not count in the end, only what you do for Jesus Christ will last.

He is so worthy; let Him move you into ministry, and be obedient to His holy will.

I guarantee you that your life will be better for it, and you will never be the same.

The Lord knows exactly what is best for you, and He never fails. Let the mind of Christ Jesus work in you always.

Put forth an effort to be more like Jesus, after all, He is the best and greatest example, any man will ever have. May your day be blessed, because of your obedience to God Our Father, which is in heaven, Amen?

## Oneness With God
(John 15:5)

You are His child

Why is it so hard to obey and do what is right? It is called flesh; it is the one thing that Christian men and women battle with every day. The flesh wants to do what the flesh wants to do, and the truth be told, on a daily basis, the flesh is the winner with a knock out in the first round with most Christians. Why? Because as a child of the Most High God most Christians are not really trying to overcome what is happening in their lives. You have a battle fighter, but you want go to Him. The Word of God gives us specific instructions on how to dress for life.

He tells us to put on the whole armor of God, (Ephesians 6:10-18). But what are you doing? You are doing exactly what the flesh wants you to do. God is not pleased with the life that you are living; and when He is not pleased He will bring His punishment upon you. He did it with the children of Israel, and He is still doing it today.

Christ did not die, on the cross, just too die; He died that we might have life, and have it more abundantly. Some Christians feel like they cannot make it; but I want to assure you, that you can. Key to it all is this, you must do it God's way; there's no getting around it.

You should be very tired of wrestling and fighting your own battles, living all kind of lifestyles; and doing any and everything each and every day that He allows you to live.

Then you step into the House of the Lord on Sunday, and sit there like a frog on a log.

Only because you have allowed yourself to be weighted down in your spirit; with the many things that is not yours to hold on too.

Don't let the things that come to you in the spirit cause you not to communicate with your Father (God).

There is nothing that you do that He does not see; there is nothing that you do that He will not forgive, so trust Him, and pull yourself together.

We have all come from something in our past; we all have skeletons in our closets, and there are some things that we will take with us to the grave.

But, He still loves you, and He still loves me.

The other problem is that man wants to punish himself well, guess what? God does not need your help with that. We will certainly and without a doubt pay for what we have done in our bodies, yes, (some are already paying), those pains and that sickness that you are going through, (punishment). But the good thing is; He is the one who say's what that punishment will be. Whatever it is, or will be, it's all-good because He knows what we need. Yes, and even when it comes to being punished, learn how to say "thank you God". If you don't have that personal relationship with Him, get it; He's waiting on you with His loving arms wide open.

## Mother To Son

(Judges 13:24; 1 Samuel 8:3; Hebrews 12:5)

Lovingly submitted

As a mother I am compelled to write this lesson concerning our young men; I pray that it will fall into the hands of every young man. God wants you to know that being a man is not about the way you dress; it is not about impressing other young men; but it is about being like your Father in heaven, who made you for a specific purpose. God values you; you are precious in His sight. I know that a lot of our young men just grew up with no adult supervision; I also know that some grew up with adult supervision and the Word of God, and that some of you were raised in the church.

But now, because of your surroundings, and the company you keep, you have strayed away. I am aware of the fact that somewhere down the road of life, the older men became uncaring about the outcome of their sons, and children period for that matter, especially in broken homes.

It does not matter if you came from a broken home or not; God loves you, and can use you. But, you have got to let go of some things.

The people of this world do not mean you any good. I have watched over the years how young men have turned to sex, drugs, gangs, and clubs.

I see how they treat the young women, I see how they attempt to do the best that they can as a parent; yet they are failing in giving real love to their children, could it be because they were never shown how to love? It is a shame before almighty God. I am not placing blame, because I am not the judge; I am just the messenger.

Some of our young men have had to face some terrible things; for instance being beat up by gangs in order to be a gang member; thinking that people are their friends when all they are doing is using them for their own purpose.

But, if you are a praying mother God will and can change all of that. The thing that we as a parent have to do is keep them before God every day, 24/7.

I know that He can and will change them, I have been praying for a lot of years for my son, and for all of yours too. I know that God has heard me and I know that He is answering my prayers, and He does it in His own time.

Young men, please hear me, it is past the time to let God have His way in your life. And to those of you who feel you don't need anybody, Oh yes you do, you need God, and you need Him right now. He is the only One who can and will fulfill you. Try Jesus, you will be glad you did.

# You Are Not As Smart As You Think You Are

(Proverbs 3:13; James 1:5; 3:15; 17)

Yes, you

You can be the smartest person in the world, and still be the biggest dummy in the world. It is not about your learned senses; it is about the word of God.

Education is good, and is very much needed; but it is nothing without the knowledge of God.

If you don't possess the wisdom of God, then you are not smart at all, sorry to have to say this, but a lot of Christians do not.

You can only get wisdom from one source, and He is God, God said if you want wisdom you are to ask Him for it, and He will give it to you.

How can I really know what it is that God would have me do in this life, unless I possess His wisdom?

We have so many people trying to tell us how to live; when all we have to do is go to the Word of God. Everything you need is within the pages of the Holy Bible.

Now, when was the last time you picked it up and when was the last time you heard from God?

There are a lot of things you would not have to deal with, if you would get into the Word and let the Word penetrate you.

I am challenging you today, began to read His Word, start with a Chapter a day.

The Gospels would be a great place to start, and when you read, read it with conviction, pray and ask the Holy Spirit to help you. Let God speak to you, because He surely will.

If you are already reading, consider doing it even more, for instance, try reading thru the Bible in one year, do your best.

The more you read, the more you will want to read; it will become a vital part of your daily walk.

God will be pleased with you, and I must say; you will also be pleased with your own self.

# Who Are You Helping?

(Acts 20:35)

No man is an island

We are called for a purpose in this life, it is not enough for us to sit back and not do anything to help someone else.

Oh, to be like Jesus, this would be a great accomplishment.

Don't be a possessor of I've got mine attitude, and let them get theirs, this is wrong.

He has not blessed you for you just to glory in yourself; He has blessed you so that you would help someone else in this life.

When you do what God has called you to do, and do it with an open mind and heart, He will get the glory.

There are people who need your help, some are people that you know, you can be of great assistance to them; but you have not because of your selfishness.

If you are a born again believer, you are failing in your trying, God's desire is that you bless someone else.

When you are obedient it brings joy, a lot of Christians think because they are up now they won't ever be down; this is far from the God's truth.

Everybody needs somebody, no man is an island, if you have the love of God, (AGAPE) it will move you; God's love places a Christian above them, your concern will be more for others, than for you, just to put it another way.

There are many ways that you can help others, and opportunity does, and will present itself.

There are people, who need a ride to the church, and they may be living right around you; what are you doing? Are you just getting in your car and going and going?

 Someone may need a kind word from you, are you able to give it? There are people sick in the hospitals, and in the prisons and nursing homes, and on and on; people need to be visited, whom have you visited lately?

These are just a few of the things that He has asked us to do; let the Lord move you into service, ask Him to show you what it is that He desires of you. Trust me, it is truly more blessed to give than to receive. Working for the Lord is an everyday toil, it's not something that you turn on and off. Now put the remote control back into His hands; for He truly is the master channel changer.

## Praise God For His Love

(Psalms 63:3-4)

Where is your desert?

We have a great opportunity today to give God the praise; we have beautiful edifices that are just awesomely done. We go in and out Sunday after Sunday and Wednesday after Wednesday; and some more often than that. How much of your going in and out is in real true praise to God?

It should not be a hard thing for you to do; after all He did give His only Son for your life; a lot of Christians have a problem with praise because they worry or wonder who is looking at them. Why do you even care? They have done nothing for you and your soul salvation.

Christian brothers and sisters, it is your time to step up to the plate, and please "Our Father", God.

David could not get to the sanctuary, but he is still praising God in these Scriptures. Your desert place may be your sick bed, or a prison cell, praise Him anyway.

There are those who cannot get to the sanctuary, but that is no excuse; because God is everywhere, and He is worthy of your praise.

Praising God brings joy, and it brings comfort to the heart of the one praising Him. It also takes you on a journey with the Lord in the spirit, He joins you in your praise; He is there with you while you are praising Him.

This is one of the greatest experiences a Christian can ever have; it is to be on one accord with the Lord.

There is much satisfaction in praising God; it gives you a real peace, and is a real comfort, just knowing that He loves you; and that you have found that same love to be in you; it is enough to make anyone give Him real true genuine praise.

If you really know Him, it will be very easy to praise Him.

Others will know that you know Him by how you praise; meaning, not just to shout; but by what comes out of your mouth on a daily basis, that's praise.

What does Christ mean to you and too your life? Is God your life? Or do you just call Him when you feel the need. I hope that it is the first part of that statement.

God is worthy to be praised; and His Love is better than life itself.

That is why you should be praising, because of the love that He has for you, for God is love. Whatever it is that you are in, or going through, remember, there is nothing greater than His love; His love conquerors all. Praise God today.

# Real True Praise

(Psalms 34)

Our God deserves just that

Aren't you glad that you are saved? How do you see Him? Is He your Lord and Savior?

God is so good to us, and He should be praised the way that He desires. The Psalmist said, I will bless the Lord at all times, and His praise shall continually be in my mouth.

What a proclamation to the Father up above. He inhabits those who praise Him.

We are His workmanship; and have been created by Him for His pleasure.

When you come into the fullness of God, don't attempt to abort your blessings, and don't turn around, there is nothing back there for you; that dear saint is a trick of the enemy, he is telling you, you are missing something, but you are not.

When we praise God it excites Him, and He blesses us in return.

When He blesses us, it does not have to be money as most would want or think.

God blesses us in so many ways, for some; He has kept away sickness, for others he has blessed their loved ones from the dangers of this world, He has even gone with you down the highways and bi-ways of life protecting you from all hurt, harm, and danger.

He even protects you when you are sleeping, from our enemy, Satan.

There is nobody like God; just knowing Him; is reason enough to give Him thanks. He is a loving kind, and compassionate Father.

It would be in your best interest to learn how to be that same way, showing love to others.

Remember this, you cannot fool Him He knows all there is to know about you.

So why not thank Him every day for His loving kindness toward you.

Praise is solely between you and God; you see it's all about Him.

If you desire to please your Father then praise is the way, and it is so ordered.

## Prayer Answered

(2 Chronicles 20:14-19; 27)

Follow your leader

This is a good day to learn and know that God is a God of His Word He cannot lie. God used the prophets of the Old Testament to show forth His mercy and His power. Today we have the man of God the Pastor / Shepherd or the Angel of the Church. When he is given instruction he gives it to the people of God.

There is only one real problem; we have Christians who do not want to obey those instructions.

I hope that you will learn from this lesson, brothers and sisters, God did not call you to lead His people, He called the Pastor. He is the only one that God gives the vision for the house.

Some pastors are not being allowed to function in their calling. You have bought a curse upon yourself, if you are one of those who block his vision and stop the work of the Lord from going forth beware, because your punishment is at hand.

If you are being disobedient; then you are out of order.

Don't be that child that is always causing problems just because you cannot have your way.

You see, it is not about you; it is about doing what the Lord is saying through your Pastor/Teacher.

There's an army of young men rising up around the world, and they are doing the work of the Lord. They are living upright lives; and they are pleasing in His sight.

You need to be very careful of what you say, and how you act toward the called man of God.

He is the one with the information that will possibly save you from yourself and a burning hell, he is the one who prays for you, when you are not even praying for yourself, he is the one who teaches you, and feeds you the unadulterated Word of Almighty God.

He is also the one who does not get the respect that he deserves, and he is the one who is talked about, and lied on.

But still he continues in obedience, doing what the Father has called Him to do.

The battle is still being fought, but the victory has already been won.

It was won on the Cross-at Calvary over two thousand years ago. The time is now and is at hand for Christians everywhere to trust in their leaders. God knows exactly what He is doing, so you stand still and see the Salvation of the Lord.

## In Him Only
(Acts 17:27-28)

How are you moving?

Christian men and women are you truly seeking God for your life; He is not so far removed that He cannot be found. If you seek Him, you will find Him.

Some Christians really do not put forth an effort to get close to God, or to find Him. They don't because they are afraid of the change that will happen in their lives.

Christian lives change for the better when God enters into the equation, this should be an open door deal.

Aren't you tired of living life your way? All you do is mess up when you try to control things. We were not created to have the wheel it belongs to Jesus Christ; we were however created for a purpose. That purpose is to praise God; He has even told us how to praise. God's love for us is unconditional.

If you don't have God in your life, you must know that you are not really living, you just exist.

You cannot do anything without His permission, when you move; it is only because He is allowing it.

Whatever you do; you do it because of His love and compassion for you.

If you are not living and moving according to His will, this can be your starting place. Most saved people cannot hear the Spirit of God speaking to them because they refuse to go into the Word, (the Bible). Those that are lost hear and ignore out of ignorance.

It is time that Christians started to live a life that is pleasing in the sight of God.

Can you not see who He is? He is God the Father, He is God the Son, He is God the Holy Ghost, and He is Master, Savior, Redeemer, Deliverer, Healer, and much, much, more. Put your trust in Him and be assured that He will bring you through.

Now think about this, a person can trust their earthly parents so easily; but they cannot trust the one who gave His all, (Jesus Christ). This is a true fact for you to digest and think about?

Everything that you have done, or will ever do, is in the hands of the Lord, and without Him, it would be utterly impossible to do anything at all.

You do know that if He desired to, He could stop you in your tracks right now right where you are? He is God, and He has got it like that. God says that, we are His offspring. You must give yourself back to Him, and you have to do it of your own free will. You have been blood bought, by Jesus Christ the Lord; no false god could do this for you. Jesus Christ is the reason that you are living and breathing this day.

# Jesus Christ Master Teacher

(St. Luke 6:27-34)

Unconditional Love

The Lord gave us specific instructions on what we are to do toward everyone even our enemies.

Let's look at what He is saying: First, He is speaking to the ones that will hear.

Isn't our Lord great, Jesus knows that there will be those who say they are His, but will still do what they desire?

Now He is lining His Word up, He say's Love your enemies; He does not make mistakes, the Lord knew you would have enemies.

Then He tells you too, do good to them that hate you; oh my, are you still there? Yes; do well unto the hater.

Now, you are to bless them that curse you; this is good. Everybody is not going to be for you or in your corner.

Oh my Lord; pray for those who mistreat you; you know that this is the right thing to do, because it frees you.

Don't retaliate; vengeance belongs to the Lord, all you are going to do is mess it up anyway.

Now, you are to also give freely; God loves a cheerful giver. And last but not least, He tells you to treat others the way that you want to be treated. This is considered to be the "Golden Rule", a truly good rule, and also the last rule.

You are to consider others more highly than yourselves; this is God's Word.

Be assured that this does work, and it also brings joy to your life, but only if you are sincere when you practice it.

When you love like the Father say's to do, you are letting the world know that you are a child of God, and that you want your life to reflect just that. You are to show Christ likeness at all times.

When you obey Him, and live according to His holy Word, then you are letting the world know; you are His child.

I know that there are those of you who would say this is hard to do. Well, it is not hard at all, if you are living your life according to the Word of God.

Think of it this way; it was not an easy thing for Jesus Christ to give up His Deity; and come and die on the Cross-for you, but He did; and He did it with the Love of His Father in mind. We are to do that very same thing, show our love, through obedience.

Their use to be a song that was sang when I was growing up, concerning love and hate, I found it to be very true. The title was and I am sure that some of you will also remember; it's a thin line between love and hate, how true.

If you really want to be obedient, break that line; and cross over to the right side. After all, Jesus has already made it easy and possible for you to do just that.

# Everything Belongs To God

(Psalms 24)

Sure enough you

It is disheartening to watch people today; and how possessive they have become. Having the attitude that everything belongs to them.

Well here is your wake-up call, everything on this earth belongs to God; including you. He is the one who spoke things into existence.

A lot of Christians have gotten caught up in this; they feel that what they have belongs to them; they do not seem to possess any empathy or sympathy for others.

This is very disturbing in the Lord's sight. You have the instruction manual (the Holy Bible), it is everywhere, it is in your homes, cars, purses, etc. It is everywhere but inside of you. Why do you refuse to read it? Could it be that you do not want to face the real truth, you see when you get in the Word of God He speaks directly to you; and anytime that God speaks there will be changes in your life. You cannot get close to God and not change; that is utterly impossible.

There is nothing wrong with having, unless you are in the mind frame that it is yours. Then it becomes wrong, because God has made you a Steward over what you possess. What you do with what He has in-trusted you with determines what type of Steward you are.

Your children do not even belong to you; when I say nothing is yours, I mean nothing.

It pleases God to give too you; but it also pleases Him even more when you give to others.

This shows Him how much you really love and trust Him.

You need to be like David and praise God, simply because you know that nothing belongs to you; but, that it all belongs to The Father.

David talks about going before the Lord a certain way, he says with clean hands, meaning, having right actions.

David also talks of a pure heart, check yourself; is your attitude right before you approach the Father. You cannot go before the throne of grace just any kind of way; for you must yield your will to the will of the Father.

God knows what is best for you, I would certainly rather yield my will too Him, than for Him to approach me for not doing so.

What I am saying is this; it is best for you to go to God, before God has to come to you. That would not be a good thing. When you truthfully seek God, with your whole heart, then He will bless you.

The King of Glory is before, won't you let Him in, and praise Him, right now for His mighty works. Hallelujah, Amen.

## Do You Believe The Good News

(St. Luke 1:19-20)

I hope you do

God is a good God; He is to be believed and trusted, most definitely by the Saints. I know there are times when things happen in your life where you may want to doubt, but, that is a dangerous thing to do.

Instead of doubting, try praying for strength to overcome whatever it is that is trying to overcome you.

There is nothing above the name of the Lord. There is no situation too big for Him. You name it, He can handle it the problem is not with God; it is with you, way deep down inside, when you fail to trust and believe that He can and will do what He said He would do.

God sent His angel, Gabriel, to assure them of the joy that was to come. This mighty archangel, Gabriel, who had stood in Almighty God's presence,

There are a lot of reasons for unbelief the main one being selfishness. Zechariah did not believe his report; and because of it the angel told him he would be dumb and not be able to speak.

God will and does punish those whom He loves; but there is always a time limit on that punishment. In the case of Zechariah the punishment was for nine months, (long time).

The angel said until the time of fullness had come, the deliverance of John.

When Elisabeth had John it all ended.

What's your time? How long will you suffer before you see Him for who He really is? He is God the Father.

Don't you be a Zechariah, doubting the message of Sovereign God?

I know God to be true to his Word, and He keeps His promises.

It is always in our best interest, don't you cause God to bring punishment down on you, all because you want to keep doing dumb things, it's not worth it, and don't you rationalize your wrong, because it does not fit.

You may think you have a good reason for your unbelief, but you certainly do not. If you know someone living this kind of life, go to them, share this Word, and let them know that the Good News has come to them today, His name is Jesus; and you are His messenger.

# A Wise Word To The Young

(Ecclesiastes 12:1)

You will not be young always

You may be young now, but there will come a day when your youth will slip away.

When we are young we tend to live our lives recklessly, we do not care about much of anything.

It is all about having fun, and enjoying ourselves, as we use to put it.

Some even say I am not hurting anybody by living the way I choose to live, I disagree, because you are hurting yourself; and you are also cheating yourself out of a great life in the Lord.

This is not something we just do by ourselves; you do have help. I think you already know by now who your help is.

If you are not giving your time to God, then whom are you spending it with? Well let me help you, the Devil himself.

You do know that it is his job to keep you going down the wrong road of life.

I know for a fact that your inner man is speaking to you; he is growing weary of the life that you are living in your flesh; problem is he cannot stop you; it has to be your choice.

This part only applies to the youth that are saved; if you are not saved and are reading this he is not at all concerned about you because he knows for the time being that he has you where he wants you.

I pray that you will realize the fact that it is never too late to get right with God, and get saved.

Christian youth; it is gap closing time, so come back in and stay. You are the only one who can make this decision concerning your life.

Fun only takes you so far; if you look back over your young life what would you see? What have you accomplished? Can you see the terrible mess that you have made, by attempting to do things all by yourself?

The first word in this Scripture is: remember; this is a command from the Lord. What are you to remember? The Psalmist plainly states, remember your creator in the days of your youth. Why? Because, you will not be young always.

Yes your mind is really sharp now, and if you desired to; you could be that sponge that is soaking up the Word of God; not just to do it, but also to do it so that you may be squeezed out on those that He has placed in your presence.

Now is the perfect time for you to pull it together, because you are the instrument that He will use, to bring others in. God will do this, as you yield your will to Him. The day is coming when you will realize how important it is for you to come into the reality that you are to reverence God, and then it will not be hard at all for you to obey His holy Word; after all, you owe Him your life, even in your youth, and He is the reason that you are here.

## The Vision

(Isaiah 6:1-9)

Isaiah saw Him

Isaiah mentions what he saw in his vision; he saw God seated on a throne, he said He was high and exalted, and the train of His robe filled the temple. God was in the house.

Have you ever had the opportunity of experiencing God in the house? It is an awesome thing.

We are now in the process of seeing the vision of our pastor come to fruition.

This is not the first time; as a matter of fact we have witnessed it many times, but this is the second and biggest part of the vision that we are witnessing. It is very exciting and awesome to have an opportunity to be involved in the process of the growth of the house of God, (people coming to Christ), causes expansion and building to take place.

Let me say it to you another way, one of my favorite ways; it is Truly Wonderful.

I am so glad that he is a man who follows God and is letting the Holy Ghost lead the way.

When God's glory is evident, it leaves no place to let anything or anyone get in your way. I know he sees God as the "Great Emancipator" of all mankind. I know that he sees Him as "Big and not small" and so do I. God wants His people to be involved, and that should be enough for all of us.

Isaiah made another statement: He said woe is me, I am undone; my lips are unclean, what a testimony.

He knew he was a sinner, and he humbly admitted it. That is what you should do, because no one is perfect. All have sinned and fallen short of the glory of God. When we are honest, then God can clean us up; there is no need to try and hide what we have done from Him. He knows anyhow; and He knows even before you commit whatever it is that you are about to do;

Is there anything in your life that you need to turn over to Jesus? If you would be honest and you should, the answer is a whopping yes.

Isaiah watched the angels praise God! Shout it out, how awesome; he saw the temple shake with the presence of God, and he saw the smoke fill the temple.

When God is present something is going to move, when God is present it will even cause you to move, you may even hear the angels praising with you, it does happen.

His presence fills us the same way that it filled the temple; that is why we need to praise Him. Somebody needs to see the Jesus in you, when Jesus is present in your life no one has to tell you, it is just something that you know.

When God cleans you up, you can believe that He is going to use you. The question was asked, who would go for us? This is referring to the presence of the Trinity God the Father, God the Son, and God the Holy Ghost. God is actually asking this question of man, and He is still asking the same question today.

Will your answer be as swift, and as quick as Isaiah's? "Here I am Lord, Send me". The same way the people needed an Isaiah in that day, somebody needs you, the question remains the same, will you go?

## We Are No Secret To The Lord

(Psalms 139:13-14)

He knows everything.

The Lord God knows all there is to know about you; after all it is He who formed you in the womb of your mother.

Nothing can be kept from Him; nothing is a secret to Him. Whether you want Him to or not, He knows you intimately, isn't that incredible?

Yes, He knows you like that, yet you do not want to know Him.

How strange that seems, for one who has been created by the Master of the entire universe.

People believe and trust in everything, and everyone but Him.

David is pleased with the Father; that is why He is praising Him.

You should do the same, and give Praise to God from whom all blessings flow.

If you've ever had the opportunity to see a newborn baby come into the world, then you should really be able to embrace what is being expressed here.

It is an experience that you will never forget; do you remember that one day you were a child?

I am reminded of the Scripture that says children are a heritage of the Lord; and happy is the man whose quiver is full. (Psalms 127)

It is amazing that David would talk about how he was made; if you read on, He says in the lower part of the earth, (the womb).

God is an awesome God, and no man or spirit will ever be able to do what He has done, fact is, that I am grateful we are blessed.

It saddens me to know how blessed we were from the very beginning of our lives, and to see where we have come. He put us together; can't you see it, we are a masterpiece that has come from God?

But, there are those who chose to abort that beautiful and blessed work, called a child.

My prayer is that God will help them to see, because they truly do not; and cannot know what they are doing. Father, I thank you today for life, because as David has so beautifully stated; we are fearfully and wonderfully made.

## Connected To The Right Person

(Acts 27:23-25)

Be sure

There are many different storms in life; the storm of depression, abuse, drugs, prostitution, adultery, fornication, lust, hate, selfishness, gossip, and etc. I could go on but you've got it.

We are living in a world where these things have come to the very surface and there is no shame.

People are being told it is okay to do whatever they want to do. They are saying it is nobody's business but yours, and that what you do is between you and God.

This is not true, it is a device of the enemy, to keep you going in the wrong direction; you are your brother's keeper, therefore you are responsible for what you do, and you are also accountable.

Christian brothers and sisters, we can help someone as we go through life, or we can hinder them, which one are you doing?

Every Christian should be striving to live a life that exemplifies the life that Jesus Christ has set in motion for us. This is the lifestyle that will be pleasing in the sight of God. It is of most importance that we get close to the right people; your very life could depend on it.

Storms can take everything that you own, but they cannot take your faith in God.

There is always going to be someone around you to help pull you through; but, it is up to you to be spirit focused and prayerful, in order to know who that someone may be.

God is always looking out for us, because He knows that even though we are His, we will still make mistakes and falter.

Let Jesus lead you, not part of the way, but, all the way, sometimes that leading will come through the help of another individual.

There is no shame in depending on someone else; the shame comes when you think that you can do everything of yourself, and by yourself. When you think like this you have already set yourself up to fail.

Trust The Holy Ghost, He will send someone your way that is caring and loving, the same as Paul was in these Scriptures. The reason is, when people care, they will reach out to others and show real true genuine Agape love. This is the Love of the Father; and His love will last forever, and ever, throughout all the ages.

# When Jesus Does It

(St. John 2:11)

It is done

How many times have you set out to do something and failed? How many times have you done something and really thought it was great, but it was not? My guess would be many. We often think of ourselves as the master planners of everything we do or come up with.

Example: women who can cook, they can't see anyone else doing it but them; no one else can do it completely to their liking, and it is the same with men.

We are all programmed to something that we feel no one else can do like us.

I know that I am right. Take a moment now and think about it. There, you see. You are still human and subject to error.

Well that is certainly where Jesus differs from us; He never erred, and He never sinned. This is just awesome to know, that we have a Savior who came into this world by the same means as we did, (born of a woman).

He walked, talked, ate, slept, and never did anything wrong.

He had compassion for those that were around Him, and for those that were far off.

He was given something to do, and He did it to the Utmost.

What about you, how are you doing in what you have been called to do?

It did not matter whether man called him upon or woman, to do whatever was needed, Jesus got the job done.

He did not stand around waiting on anyone else to come along and do what was His to do.

He did not sit around and sulk because His disciples were not helping Him to do what had to be done, He just did it.

He got the job done, and it was always done satisfactorily.

As a matter of fact He did it so well, no one else would even dare try.

There was no one then, and there never will be anyone who is worthy enough to do what Jesus did.

Jesus took it all the way to the cross, and that is where He left it; that is where they were meant to be, (the sins of mankind).

Want you thank Him today, for a job well done; if there is anything that you know you have left undone, this would be a good time to finish it.

## God's Family
(Ephesians 3:15)

We are His

Every family that is functioning in this world has come about because of an earthly father. Every earthly father has not earned the right to be called father even though he has played a big part in someone's being here.

There is more to being a father than the part a man plays in a child being born!

We should give honor to our earthly father, and this is good, and very good. But there is one who is greater than him!

God is our heavenly Father; first and foremost, it all began in heaven with Him.

I am so thankful that He loves us enough to give us an opportunity, to be born into this world, and to be able to function, and do as much as we possibly can in His holy name.

I wonder how many of us ever think about the fact that God is your Heavenly Father. How much attention are you giving to Him? I really don't have to ask you about your earthly father, because I already know that if he is living, and has raised you, well, you are there for him.

It should be the same way with the Lord, even more so, because He is to be adored, praised, and given the utmost attention. We are to call Him at all times, and love on Him every day.

The Father loves you so very much it should not be hard for you to love Him back,

He desires your presence before Him; God gets so much joy when we come to the throne of grace, it excites Him.

I think about the fact that I am so undeserving, I have done nothing at all for Him to love me the way that He does; yet He just keeps on loving me, and making a way for me, and, you also.

We have this same opportunity today, to love our families the same way, unconditionally.

It is not good to try and make people live their lives the way you think they should, especially when you are not doing so great with your own.

I thank God that He looks beyond our faults and sees our needs.

How great it would be if we saw our families the way that our Father in heaven sees us.

What a great world it would be, if we would just live our lives the way that our Father desires. If you are having problems in your family circle turn it over to the Lord, and watch Him work it out.

A word of caution to those who want things to happen right away, God's timing is not our timing, so be patient, and wait on your change.

# What Is Your Mind Set On?

(Colossians 3:2)

Fix It

We are to have control over the things of our minds; we are not to let our mind have control over us.

The mind can do some strange things, and cause us to think in some very strange ways. Most of the way that we think is earthly. Now why is that?

Because you are a human and you are first carnal (flesh). As a Christian you have got to begin to live your life in the spirit of the Lord that is most important to our stay here on this earth.

Even though we are in this world, we are not to be like those of the world.

When you gave your life to Jesus Christ, some changes had to be made concerning you. There has to be a transition into this new life, Paul told the Colossian believers to set their minds on heavenly things over the earthly things.

Earthly things are temporary; and they are going to perish one day.

Therefore we need to home in on those things that will take us to eternity.

The number one thing that a Christian needs to focus on is the Word of God.

We need to Study His Word each and every day, we need to be in mediation at all times, we need to keep our prayer life alive, by staying constantly before the throne of grace.

When we do these things on a daily basis, then the enemy cannot confuse us, or lead us in the wrong direction.

Most of the time, people are doing the things that they desire to do; and are saying without batting an eye, that God told us to do it.

You know for sure in your heart when you do this, that you have told a lie, and not just a lie; you have lied on God.

You have got to learn how to get a hold of yourselves and be truthful about what's really going on, because the truth is what God loves.

Telling the truth is the best thing that a man or woman can ever do for themselves, after all; God already knows, He just wants to hear you say it.

# Natural Desires vs. Spiritual Desires

(Romans 8:8-9)

Which are you doing?

An unsaved person cares only for self, he or she is not worried about anyone else, and nothing else matters to him or her.

They do not care about God, and they certainly don't care about you.

You may be experiencing this in your family life, or with a friend, and maybe even an enemy.

We see this constantly in the world of the stars; it is not all of them, but it is the vast majority. They believe that where they are, that they arrived there on their own. A lot of their beliefs are in a man created religion.

This is a religion that is taking them straight into hell.

The exact opposite is true of those who live according to the Spirit; they are living a life that is pleasing in the sight of God.

We must keep our mind set on the things of the Spirit, for He is the one who leads and guides us into all truth; He is God, The Holy Ghost.

He will do it for everyone who admits that he is a sinner, and who will believe in the Resurrection of Jesus, and Confess that Jesus died on the Cross, and rose for your sins.

*Scattered Thoughts*

The natural man will never do what God wants him to do; he has a mind of his own.

The natural man loves to do sinful things, and he loves to hurt and destroy others.

The spirit man loves to do what the Spirit of God say's to do.

The only ones that will obey the Spirit of God are the ones who have been saved and sanctified, (set apart) to live a holy life before the Father.

God is a loving and forgiving God, but He will not wait on you forever.

He gives every man and woman ample time to change their lives for the better.

The sinful mind leads you to a place of no return, and an eternity of final damnation (permanent).

The saved man is led of the Holy Spirit into eternity to live with the Lord, forever, (permanent).

Which one is more pleasing to you? My prayer is that it will be the latter one.

Why live a life of fighting with the flesh each and every day, when all you have to do is turn it over to Jesus. After all, He has already fought and won the battle for you; He did it over two thousand years ago, at the Cross. What will be your decision, and what will you submit to today, the Natural desires or the Spiritual desires? Only you have the answer to that. True believers of God, don't you turn back and believe in your sin nature again.

You have come too far to turn around, go forward.

## Most Gracious
(St. John 3:16)

God Is

There is nothing that you or I can ever do to top what God has done for us.

He is so loving, so generous, so kind, and so forgiving. We could never do anything that would cause us to step up to this place.

There are a lot of kind people in this world, but they cannot compare to the Lord, and what He has done for us, and are still doing for all mankind.

Man's love comes with conditions, almost always. I do something for you; then I look for you to do something for me. Oh my, I know that I am right.

God is not like that, His love is unconditional, aren't you glad? I sure am.

When I sit down and think of how He has blessed my family and myself, I give Him a Hallelujah praise, (the highest praise), because He is so deserving of it.

A lot of Christians take God for granted, your clock is ticking, and you need to move from here. What do you do when He blesses you?

I often observe people when we go out to eat; how they come into the restaurant, get their food, sit down, and bend over the plate and go for it. You don't know what you are consuming.

If you are a child of God, then you need to show an outward expression of grace for what you are about to receive, (Romans 14:6).

Others need to know, who do not know, that Jesus is, and that He is worthy.

But how will they know unless those of us who profess to know Him begin to show it to the world, because He is truly worthy.

Some Christians cannot even express it to their own family members, because they are afraid of what they might think of them.

Good Lord; you worry about them, well, what about Jesus? He is the one that you should be concentrating on, praising, and becoming more like.

We have an opportunity to help turn this world around, and when people see you doing these acts of praise; it will make them curious, and they will come to you, or they will find someone else that they can ask, why do you Christians do what you do, that Loving God, praying and praising Him thing? This will be your opportunity to lead someone to Christ.

# The Day The World Got A Major Overhaul

(Genesis 1)

God spoke.

When God speaks things happen just because He is an "Awesome God". God called forth heavens, and also the earth

God said let there be. The Spirit of God, (God the Holy Ghost) moved upon the face of the water and caused it to divide.

He spoke to a dark world that was once without form and void; He said let there be and it was so.

The darkness became light, because He divided it into two parts; He called one night, and the other day.

The sun was by day, (the greater light) and the moon was by night, (the lesser light).

These stars give light to the earth still today, such beauty and splendor for us to behold.

The waters were separated by expansion, they were divided and there was dry land.

The trees were set in their places, trees of every kind, fruit trees, etc. The herbs were called forth; the mountains came forth.

The stars joined the sun and the moon in the sky, their purpose; that you would be able to tell the different seasons of the year.

God created the beast of the sea, and every living creature on the earth.

He created the cattle, the fowl of the air, creeping things each of their own kind.

His plan is a perfect plan. On the same day that He formed the creatures He put air on the earth

What had once been nothing but darkness, in a moment became something, by Almighty God.

He included man here to, because on the sixth day He created Adam after His image, and His likeness.

Then God put Adam to sleep, and Eve was made from his rib, this was the first operation.

He gave Adam and Eve complete control over everything that He had made.

What an Awesome God, what a Loving God. As God spoke things into existence in the first five days He called it good. The sixth day when He made man He called it very good. This lets us know that God loves us and that we are very important to Him. Now that you know, who and what is He to you?

## The Gift That Just Keeps On Giving

(Mark 2:17)

Jesus

You cannot beat Jesus giving no matter how hard you try; no matter what you accomplish in this life. That is all that it will be, an accomplishment.

Jesus Christ is so worthy of our praise. But does He really get it.

We celebrate several times of the year the Savior of the world; saying that we are honoring and praising Him for His mighty blessings.

They are His Birth, His Life, His Death, and His Resurrection.

Are you really showing Him the gratitude that He truly deserves?

As I write this page we are in the process of getting ready to celebrate another Christmas. Well brothers and sisters my question to you is this; is it really about Jesus? Only you know.

As I look around at the people moving about buying there different gifts and listen to the news reports, what I am hearing and seeing is just the opposite.

I see people buying this and that; I hear about the fights over certain games and etc.

I have even heard of people getting hurt and maimed trying to get into stores before others. There is nothing wrong with buying something for someone you love; the wrong is in the fact that Jesus Christ is being left completely out.

He is the one who gave His life for you; so that you would be able to have the life that you now live and enjoy.

How much of your time are you spending in church services, (the work of the church)? Are you giving to organizations that are reaching out to the poor?

The gift that He gave to us was unconditional, (Himself).

He came, He taught, and He showed us how to live our lives in Him.

Then He went back to His Father in heaven; because He knew His job here on earth was done. Now, the rest is left up to you; it is past wake up time, He gave; now you give.

## Your Time Is Running Out

(Joshua 24:15; Luke 4:8)

Choose today

Joshua said it best, when He said; as for my house and me we will serve the Lord. Just whom are you serving?

The time for you is running out! People have become so unconcerned about their soul salvation.

We are living in a day and time when things are just what they are things. Nothing is important; it is all about doing your own thing.

Well I must caution you here, your own thing may be about to send you straight to hell.

Christian people we have got to keep our hearts and minds stayed on Jesus.

There are many who want to still live the way they did before they were saved.

But, God has called you out for a reason; someone has to come to Christ through you.

But how can they when they are watching you, each and every day, doing what you want to do, instead of what the Lord is saying you should be doing?

Christian men still want to play the field, and I am not talking about baseball; Christian women still wanting to flirt, and are doing it, skirts are going up higher and higher. How long will you play your game before you get some sense spiritually?

The way that you let go is get into the Word of God, read, study, and meditate daily; it is a must if your life is going to change for the better you give.

You may not realize it but you are leading someone, but where you are leading them, only you know, they have put their trust in you, and God is watching you.

Live your life each day as though it was your very last, live it to the fullest, but live it the way that God would have you live it. How will you do this?

The more you get into Jesus the more He will get into you, it's in His Word, that is where He speaks, that is where you will find your deliverance, (the Bible).

Do it so that those who are around you will see and know that truly He is God.

Don't be a stumbling block to those who look up to you, how sad it would be that you make it into heaven because you are saved; and because someone else is to go into an eternal hell forever and ever.

Be very careful and be thoughtful, because it could be your mother, father, sister, brother, friends, or children. Because forever is a long time to be without God, and remember, someone is watching you; and you will reap what you sow!

## Take It Up With God

(Leviticus 20:7; Romans 8:38-39)

Be careful of what you say

Isn't it ironic how people have no respect for anything or anyone anymore?

But today there is still a remnant of saved people who love the Lord and want to live according to His holy will.

There are churches today that are giving out of their hearts to those who they feel led to give to. We should Praise God for them.

But what do you do when your giving backfires? I am so glad that you asked.

The answer is: you give it to Jesus; He is the only one who can and will handle it.

The Word tells us that vengeance belongs to God.

I am so glad that I learned this at an early age, because people will hurt you; and they will do it on purpose.

This is the evil man (Satan), which they allow to have his way on the inside of them.

People of the world are never going to act right, because it is not in their nature to do so.

As a matter of fact, saved people are not always going to act right either.

This is why the Lord God left us with forgiveness; the asking to be forgiven and the actual act of forgiving others, forgiveness is the way; it frees you so that you may be used by God.

The Lord is telling us that if we do not forgive, neither will He forgive us before His Father, which is in heaven.

I do not care what it is, or who did it, as a Christian you must forgive them.

I don't know about you, but there is no one on this earth, or anywhere else for that matter that can stop me from obeying God's Word.

I certainly do not want the Lord to turn His back on me before Our Father in heaven. Things are going to happen in our lives, and as a Christian; you must realize that they come for your growth, and they come to make you strong. These are the trials of life.

It does not matter whether it happens to you as a family, a church family, or as an individual, it is coming your way, so get ready.

What you have to do is let the Lord have it, you will be glad that you did. This is a good day to grow-up in the Spirit of the Lord.

## No Shame

(Genesis 19:1-11; Leviticus 18:22; 20:13; Judges 19:22; Romans 1:26-27; 1 Corinthians 6:9.)

The forbidden things

Sodomy has become an acceptable lifestyle in our world today. Yet the Word of God tells us that your own blood is upon you, and you shall die. There is no life in this death stated here.

We see man and man, and woman and woman, carrying on with one another like a man and a woman.

It is all over the television, on movie screens, etc. It has gotten so vile here in the United States that you have Judges marrying same sexes, laws are being passed for them in each of the States, while they are constantly trying to remove God.

It really does not matter what man does, or thinks because one day it is going to end, when it goes before the *Soul Judge*, The Lord God Almighty.

It is an abomination in His sight. There is no shame anymore whatsoever in the ones who are committing these horrible acts; as a matter of fact they feel there is nothing wrong with it.

You have to watch what you embrace; God despises it, and as a Christian so do I.

(I am speaking of the sin, not the person). My place and yours is to pray, pray that those who are living this lifestyle will see that it is ugly and wrong, pray that they will change before God turns them over to it.

We always protect what we deem to be right, and wrong is going to always be with those who speak against what they feel is right.

We have seen homes broken up over this; we see and hear of people dying daily for the desires of the flesh.

Some who are innocent are being dragged into this because of their partners.

If you are married and committing this act, you are taking this home to your spouse, the one who you vowed to love and cherish forever. God has said your own blood is upon you, you shall die, and it is happening; we call it *AIDS*, God's word is truth.

What God says always come to pass; it makes no difference if you believe it or not.

My prayer is that as you read these Scriptures, that you will let them penetrate to your very soul, let them take root inside you, let them minister to you, and; ask God to help you. We all know of someone that is in this situation, our place in this is to pray for them.

Today the Lord God is giving you an opportunity to be a witness to someone that you love and care about. You don't have to say a word unless He leads you to do so; give these anointed words to them and let the Holy Ghost do the rest.

When we come into the knowledge of a thing, and we do all of the time, it should help us to do better.

I sincerely believe that there are those who are seeking

to be free from this curse.

I also believe that God has anointed me to write it, for such a time as this, and the glory belongs to God.

## Admonished to Love Everyone
(Hebrews 13:1-2)

But do we?

God has called the Christian man, woman, boy and girl into greater things.

As a child of God you are required to live a certain lifestyle; you are to be Christ-like.

No man or woman has ever given their life to the Lord and remained the same, it is utterly impossible.

The Author of Hebrews starts off this chapter by saying we are to have brotherly love for one another.

God is growing His churches all over the Nation and World.

He expects us to be on our best behavior so that we can draw others.

The Lord God knows us so well that He tells us not to be forgetful toward strangers; He says that we are to show them love.

He even goes on to explain what is happening, He tells us that by forgetting some, not all; that we have entertained angels.

It is a good thing to have the spirit of friendliness.

Have you ever thought about the fact that someone along the way has done the same thing for you?

You have not always been around just the people that you know; all of us have met strangers along the way.

If we show ourselves friendly, then we will in turn find a friend.

I thank God today that He did the same thing for us through His son Jesus Christ.

What an Awesome friend He is to all that will allow Him to be.

He is a friend so great, that He gave His life for us; you can't beat it even if you tried.

This is also a personal kindness that you can afford to someone else, other than those that you already know.

Christ did, He took it from brother to stranger. He is letting us know that everybody is important in the eyes of the Father.

If they are important to God, then they should also be important to you.

You now have all that you need to go forward, show yourself friendly to someone today, and do it the Christ-like way?

## Whole Again

(St. Mark 10:46-52)

Now I can see

Here a blind man called Bartimaeus gets excited because he heard Jesus was coming his way. He shouted out the name of the Lord in a loud voice and asks for mercy.

Has Jesus ever come your way and you missed Him?

Today He is giving you another chance to recognize who He is.

Some people have their sight, but are spiritually blind; they are blind to the fact that they need Him more now than ever before. They need Him to show them the way. They are also blind to the fact that He is the Son of God, and they are blind to the fact that He is their Savior and Lord.

They cannot see why a person chooses to be loud when they praise God, and they don't understand why they dance and shout to the praise of His holy name.

Well, could it be that you know the Lord; but have not allowed Him to have complete control of your heart? After all this is where He belongs. A born again person should readily submit their will to Jesus, because God is good, and He is worthy to be praised.

It should not matter who it is that He is blessing, if you are present, then you should praise with them. Try getting excited when Jesus is blessing someone other than you, you will enjoy it!

It is not surprising how they reacted at first, they tried to quiet Him; and then when Jesus said bring him to me, their whole attitudes changed.

They became as we often say, the ushers of the house, they prompted him to get up and come to Jesus.

A lot of people come and go in the church, what is happening is, they have never really come to know "The Lord God" for who He truly is; they have become spiritual busy bodies, all they do is sit and watch as He moves on others.

They are just going through the motions, they are doubters and they are gossiping about how they believe it should be. You will never get you to your healing with this attitude; you have got to be real and sincere about what you do in the name Jesus.

The blind man got up with joy in his heart, anticipating his healing; he was so happy that he got up and threw his outer garment away from himself (he had been using it to collect his money) after all he was a blind beggar.

This is how we should be as Christians; anything that gets between my blessing and me has to go.

I believe God, I believe that when He says move, you ought to move, and move quickly.

Don't you ever be afraid to tell Jesus what it is that you desire of Him.

After all this is why He is here, Bartimaeus quickly told the Lord, I want my sight; and as fast as he spoke it, the Lord granted it. He was amazingly and quickly healed, it was because of His faith. Children of God when Jesus heals you, you are healed. The key to any blessing is this, you must believe, in order to receive. You have to know without a shadow of a doubt that Jesus is who He says He is, and then you can truly say; Jesus, Son of David, have mercy on me. So keep on crying, shouting and praising, because Jesus is on His way to you.

*Scattered Thoughts*

# It's Not Your Business

(St. Mark 11:28; 33.)

Jesus' Authority

We are always sticking our noses where they do not belong. Someone always has their group together; and from that group they will get someone to go and do their dirt. It's usually the one that they feel is strong and will not have a problem with speaking what they want said.

The Sanhedrin was a sect of well-educated people; they knew the law, they were guardians over Israel's religious life. They wanted to know some things about Jesus, so they sent representatives to ask Him two questions.

One was what is the nature of your authority? The other was who was His source? People question us today when we try to buy or purchase something.

They want to know about your credentials, your credit worthiness, and they also want to know who authorized you to do what you are doing, especially if you are dealing with a bank. These people were upset, because Jesus had come to town; and He had put the moneychangers out of the temple the day before.

They had no clue that Jesus was the Messiah, because He had not yet revealed it! Their questions let us know they did not know who He was, because when you know who He is, you have no need to ask.

Jesus always answered a question with a question; you have got to love that.

How can you trap the Lord? He made His answer depend on theirs.

His question to them was concerning John the Baptist and his baptism.

Jesus ask them who is it from? Is it from God, or is it from man? Isn't this just like the Lord? I like labeling this part "get somewhere and sit down"!

Now the ball is in their court, whatever they said about John would determine who Jesus really is, okay.

They would not give the right answer about John; because they knew if they did, that they would have to say the same about Jesus.

They knew that God ordained John, but because of their unbelief about Jesus they held back.

They also feared what the people would do to them. They regarded John as a genuine prophet; yet they would not say it. The people viewed Jesus the same way (St. Matthew 21:42) that is why they feared them.

Sometimes we bring things upon our own selves, by thinking that we have it covered; and that we are too smart to be beat! This is not so; because we are not, if you are trying to play Jesus, then you are already beat. Look at this smart group of men being defeated, in the end, they said they did not know; oh yes they did. They chose to play dumb in order to look good, but they really did not. What they actually did was ended up rejecting who they really believed in, which was John. They put him alongside Jesus, therefore ending up rejecting both, just to save face. Have you rejected Him lately? If so, repent, and come back to Him, you need Him now, and forever.

# A Blessed Nation

(Psalm 66:1-12)

The Nation that praises God

This is another Psalm of thanksgiving to the Lord. In the first twelve verses the writer speaks of (us and our), in the latter verses he speaks of (I, Me, and my).

He is speaking to nations everywhere, as you know God is no respecter of persons (Acts 10:34).

He loves everybody; it is His desire that all men be saved. The author is also speaking to God; we all need to do this; when was the last time you had a conversation with your Father?

As Christians we should be constant in prayer for our nation. She is in grave trouble; God told us that we are to pray for our leaders.

We see trouble everywhere; and in every State, what are we doing to counter act it?

We see the war going on in the distant lands; no, we cannot all be there physically; but we certainly can spiritually. Prayer is what changes things, and situations; each and every day. The writer urges us to praise God with our mouths, with shouting, with singing, and with speaking.

We are to be joyful because of what God has already done; He has done great things and He continues to do so.

Praise the Lord for all that He has done.

When God works, the enemy pulls back; because he knows he has no power.

Trust God to bring you through whatever you are dealing with, and let it go. When we let go; He works. He hears us, and He knows when we are for real.

God's work is truly awesome; He has proven Himself time and time again.

He brought Moses and the children of Israel through many, many, many times.

Every time they got into a situation and went as far as they could go, God was there to deliver them.

His plan is a perfect one, He has never failed, nor will He ever.

Fact is, that we don't even have to plan; all we need to do is trust in His holy Word,

For He is Sovereign God!

He will always come out on top. People everywhere need to be aware that they are doing nothing of their own power.

It is by His power that you do what you are able to do, He rules forever and ever.

He will do away with the evil people of this world in His own time; that's His word; and that is His promise.

We are to bless Him at all times, for His wondrous works; God has preserved us for such a time as this. God has blessed us beyond our wildest belief; even on this earth we are being abundantly blessed.

He has bought us, not a mighty long way as we use to righteously sing. But, He has bought us all the way. Can you say today that it is God who has bought you? I sure can, Praise you Lord for your mighty acts. Amen.

*Scattered Thoughts*

## Anger Management

(Ecclesiastes 7:9; Ephesians 4:6)

A control issue

The Word of God is to the point about anger.

Yet we find ourselves falling into this forbidden sin time after time.

Anger can mess you up, if you are not careful it will take you to places that you really don't want to go.

Anger has caused people to lose their freedom; it has caused people to place blame everywhere but where the blame belongs. There is anger in the world today; that is called misdirected anger; it is the one where a person gets upset with everybody but himself or herself.

They choose an individual or individuals to direct it to.

I believe that if you look into yourself, you will find that it is not anyone around you with a problem, but that the problem lies within you. What you have done is allowed the devil to come into your heart, and you are giving him complete control over you. You have the power as a child of God to take it back. This is the only way that you will be delivered; you have to face the truth.

God knows what you are going through, and He's waiting with open arms to comfort and help you, the rest will be up to you. Anger can also mess with your body; it can cause all kinds of sicknesses.

That headache that you have; that won't go away, anger, that stomach problem that you just cannot get to leave, anger, and there are many more. Do not continue to give your power over to the enemy, (the devil) you see, he has no place within you, because you belong to God.

The Lord wants you to be well and in good health; the devil on the other hand wants to destroy you.

Whom will you go with? Only you know.

I can truthfully say myself that this has been one of my greatest struggles; but God, He brought me through.

I have learned how to let go of the pain and the hurt; you see, the truth is, it was no fun at all for me to be angry.

Anger also gets in the way of the work that you can be doing in the name of Jesus. Another way to look at this is that when you are angry beyond control, you have given control over to whom you are angry with. They may never know it, but you sure do. Well, if you did not know before reading this, you certainly know it now, "So just let it go". By doing this you will free yourself.

Christ said, don't let the sun go down on your wrath, so deal with your anger; and do it in a timely manner; because if you do not, you will get up each time with more added to you; and you will be even more angrier than you were when the cycle first began. So discuss it, pray about it, and even consult your pastor or leaders concerning it. Do not let it give birth to full blown sin. This is how the devil gets his foot in the door; by your not dealing with it, and if he gets his foot in, then he knows he can go even farther, be assured that anger really does rest in the bosom of fools, not the children of God.

## Who Is My Family?

(Mark 3:31-35)

Those who do His will

A lot of family members have been offended by the Christian growth of a loved one. They do not understand at the time what is taking place; they do not like the change that they see in their love one.

Even though they know that the change is genuine, it matters not to them, they want that person back to the way that they knew them.

That is not going to happen when Jesus comes into the life of an individual and changes them; that change becomes permanent.

It's amazing how we can get jealous even over things like this.

When Jesus family sent through the crowd for Him, they got a rude awaking; they found out that the world did not revolve around only them; they found out that He really was who He had professed to be, "The Son of God". They also found out that His family was way bigger than they could ever imagine, because it consisted of people of the entire world. You should be glad?

They did not have the influence over Him that they believed they possessed.

You know how it's done, even now; you say let me talk to them they will listen to me. Well, I beg to differ, if Jesus has come into that life, and they have surrendered their life too Him, there is nothing that you can do to change it.

There is really nothing to be jealous of; every man and woman has a time in their life that God will call them out of the world, and into total service, and they will obey the call.

My prayer is; that when He does call, you will be close enough to Him; that you will hear and answer.

Jesus was not putting His family down, and neither should we ours.

He was just letting them know that He had a family beyond them, a family that had been called by Him, and was being trained by Him, in the Word of God. He was preparing them to do the work of the Father, (God).

That is why His Mother and brothers were standing outside while the disciples sat in a circle around His feet.

Jesus was attesting to the fact that their relationship to Him went past our natural family ties, it was a spiritual relationship and it was real.

## The Church Belongs To God

(1 Corinthians 1:2)

Not to man

It is time that the people of God realize and recognize who the church belongs to. When this finally hits home in those who are of the idea that they have been called to be some kind of boss or whatever, then God's churches are going to grow.

God has called you to a position of sanctification in Him, through His Son Jesus Christ.

When you received Christ there was a shifting in your life, you are no longer carnal (flesh) but spiritual.

If you are still fussing and fighting with one another you have a big problem because God is not in it.

People of God it is time you learn how to submit to the powers over you, because

God is a God of order.

You cannot rule over the Pastor/Shepherd; he has been called by God to do the teaching and preaching in the house. He is also the one that God gives the vision for the church.

He cannot do what he has been called to do if he is constantly trying to keep peace in the body, and is constantly on lock down. He is the only one that God has called to pray for your soul, daily.

Don't keep letting the devil have place in your life, you have got to show him that he has no power over you because he really does not. The only reason that he does is because you are giving it to him.

If you are saved and sanctified, and I pray that you are, you will not be involved in things that may cause division in the house of God.

You have an obligation as a child of God to help keep peace in His house.

We have been set apart, (sanctified) by God; and people of non-decision (sinners), should be able to see that, don't be a fool or a stumbling block.

When the sinner enters in they should be able to see a difference in you, not just on Sunday, but every day.

Your life should always exemplify Christ, regardless of position.

When Christians come to realize that a position is nothing compared to doing what God wants us to do, then and only then will things fall into place.

We are His possessions, to do with as He pleases; we are His servants.

Therefore we who are Christians must come together in unity, because unity is important, and it is most needed in the body of Christ, and it is not to be ignored.

## So Impatient

(Jonah 4:1-3)

He prayed

There's some Jonah in all of us; we are very good at seeing it in others, but what about you? All of us have been hardheaded and hardhearted somewhere along life's way.

Jonah prayed to God about what he did not want to do.

He was very angry; we have all been there. Here are a couple of examples: we would say something like this; she made me so mad, I wanted to break her little neck. Girl I was hot, I wanted to knock his head off, (anger).

God wanted to use Jonah to deliver the people of Nineveh; He chose him, but Jonah did not feel that they should be delivered. Wait now, before you go to pointing your finger at Jonah; you have been there to, yes, and some of you are still there.

There have been times when you felt like someone was not worthy of being blessed.

You have not always been saved and filled with the Holy Ghost.

God has called you to make amends with someone but what did you do?

I know, you have said in your spirit, I know that can't be the Lord wanting me to go to that person who has hurt me, or lied on me. But it was the Lord, can you see how easy it is to reason within yourself when you do not want to obey.

The truth be told, some of you do not want to do it even now; but you say you love the Lord and have been changed.

What I like about Jonah is the fact that he was honest about how he felt. This is truly a good example for you and me.

Jonah did not want these people to receive deliverance; this is what you do when you sit in judgment over one who comes to Christ from their sinful life. So stop judging, you really don't know people as well as you think that you do! Did you forget you came from one to, a sinful life? Grace has been afforded to everyone; the people of Nineveh were more ready to accept the grace of God than Jonah was.

Anger can take you to a place that you really don't need to be, within yourself; it will cause you to not have compassion for others, and it will put you in a selfish state of mind. Jonah's worse fears came to life; he did not want God to save these evil people from themselves, but God did it anyway. He did it out of the love and compassion that He had for them.

I am so glad that God is a loving God; I am so glad that He does not listen to the voices of His stubborn children, those who want to have things their way. Why? Because if He did, there's a possibility that you and I would not have a place in the Kingdom. We should be concerned about everyone, no matter what his or her lifestyle. God can and will change anybody, that is open to being changed. (He will not force Himself on anyone).

There are those who would rather see you go down into the pits of hell, but thanks be to the Father in heaven, that is not going to happen. Bless you Lord God, for your tender Mercies.

## Is Your Flesh Burning?

(1 Corinthians 7:2)

Pleasure verses obedience

The Word of God has everything that we will ever need to make it in this world; there are rules and there are regulations as to how we are to live.

He has given us specific rules about sexual intercourse, marriage, etc.

You do not have to be a rocket scientist to know that if you are a Christian and are not married you are not to indulge in the act of sex.

Even though we know, it is still going on. We also know that everyone who is having sexual intercourse is not a sinner; the world says it is all right, so people do it.

I think that if Christian people would really take this to heart they would not be so quick to get caught up in this act, and could actually help to change the evil ways of this world.

I believe that if you would really give thought to what God wants for you, you would be able to walk away from the person that is seducing you.

Do you really know what you are doing? How does it happen? The devil knows what you like, so he gets busy, because he wants to get you off track. Don't you fall into his foolishness; you are almost where God desires you to be in Him.

When you fall prey to this burning desire in your flesh, it destroys all that you have worked so hard to accomplish, keeping yourself pure before the Lord. It also causes you to commit an act against your own body, and against God.

Our bodies are to be cherished and taken care of; if you would just be faithful and hold on, you will have whom God has for you.

But when you do not obey and continue to do things your way, understand that you have gotten in God's way.

Another way to look at this is; that, that spouse that God has chosen for you may have just passed you by, why? Because you got caught up in your own lust, do you know that your body is the temple of the Holy Ghost? If this is moving you, know this fact, you can change, and be assured that the Lord loves you, but He hates your sin.

You can ask Him now for forgiveness, and turn your life around; you were not saved to continue doing what you choose to do. Let the Lord have His way in your life, and you will be glad that you did.

## Work It Out
(Philippians 2:12)

It's up to you

Jesus Christ obeyed His Father, and carried out His every command.

We as Children of God must and should; do the exact same thing.

God has put something inside all of us that only we can accomplish, no one else can do it, the question is before you now, will you be obedient to what you hear the Father telling you to do, or will you continue to do what you want to do?

First and foremost what we are to do in this life once we become saved is obey. We have to become submissive to the will of God and to the leaders that are over us.

If you are married it even goes a step farther, you have to be submissive to your husband. Singles you are not getting by because you say you are alone; you must be submissive to the Holy Ghost.

You see, we all have to follow someone else; Paul said we are to work out our own salvation.

A lot of Christians follow as long as they are around someone they are trying to impress; but what about when you are not?

You have to realize and know that God sees every move that you make, you cannot; and are not fooling Him.

Sometimes we have to be reminded of who we are, and what we should be about; that is why Paul cautioned them in (Philippians 1:27).

As children of God we are to work out our own salvation; that's personal. No one else can do this for you.

By following the instructions left by Jesus Christ, the church will be able to work out its own problems.

All we have to do is stay prayed up, and be sincere; then God will do the rest.

We are not to worry about what people are saying about us because when you get caught up in that you will not hear God.

God has given you salvation; He did not say work for it, He said work it out. He even tells us how, with fear and trembling; I see this as being humble before the Lord; and caring for others above you.

The Lord God sees all, knows all, and is everywhere present. This should be enough for you to keep on keeping on.

It is not hard to work out problems when you turn it over to the Lord.

What happens when you do not obey? It staggers your growth in Him.

We are going to always have something in our lives that is going to keep us standing on our toes; that's okay, as long as you know that it is in the Hands of the Lord.

Now, you need to trust Him, because He is the one who is going to see you through; and believe me, He will. Nothing is too hard for God, so go ahead and face your problems head on, because you are not alone.

## Brotherly Love

(1 John 4:20)

Don't lie now

Be careful of how we use this wonderful word called love, some use it so un-caringly!

People have also taken this word love to another level a wrong one, they are teaching you by what you see; they say that it is alright to hate and not to forgive, no it is not. You see it on the television, and in movies, you hear it mentioned in songs and etc.

But what do they really mean? For years people have said this word to one another time after time, day after day.

Many people have taken it out of context; some even use it to get to the top, only to find out, that this was not where they really wanted to be.

There is another twist to this word; he speaks about the love of a brother; could it be the love of brother or sister born of the same mother?

This love that he is speaking of is the love that we should possess toward our brothers and sisters in the house of God.

Some would say it is easy to love their family members; then some would say it is not. Some would say the same about their church family.

But what do they really mean? Some say that they love Jesus, but cannot love and forgive those that they are around on a daily basis.

Believe me when I tell you, that if you cannot love those that you are around, then you are living a lie.

I love John for this one, because the people of God try to get off too easy.

He did not mind sticking you where it would hurt, which is most needed in the life of a Christian.

Now that you are aware of the fact that you can't love God, without loving your fellowman; maybe you will try and do better, my prayer is that you will.

There are a lot of people that I would choose not to love, if I controlled me, but I do not.

I choose to love them because I have the greatest love in the world, the love of Jesus Christ; the one who died that we might live.

There is nothing in this world that is going to cause me to be separated from my Father in heaven, and you should feel the same way.

A lot of people cannot get to this place in their life because of hurt feelings and jealously; it's time to let that stuff go; because that is all that it is, stuff.

Don't let the devil keep you in spiritual bondage, all of your days here on the earth, your time is too valuable, and it is too short. People are leaving here in droves; you need to redirect your attention to where it should be, and watch the Lord work it out for you. Just ask Him to forgive you, and He will. Live your life for Him, this is all that matters. You cannot love God and leave your brother out that is being unreal and false. This is the Word of God, so don't continue living a false life and be a liar to.

## A Good Wife

(Proverbs 18:22)

Let him find you.

Single Christian man, God has left explicit instructions as to how you are to obtain a wife.

He even goes on to say, that a man who finds his wife finds a good thing; and the favor of God is upon him.

You are not left alone in your quest when you seek out your soul mate because God already knows who she is.

You must be careful and prayerful in this search, and let the Lord lead you and guide you to her.

When you find her she will be suitable for you; and you will definitely and without a doubt know that she's the one.

(Proverbs 31:10) describes her well, she will be a woman of virtue, she will not pursue you, but you are to pursue her, which is good.

I feel in my heart that this is the way that God meant it to be from the very beginning.

We live in a world today where the woman does not see it this way at all?

She is living in her own world, and has her own standards about what she wants in a man. She is not the least concerned about what God has fashioned for her.

That is why you have to be prayerful in your search; God will not lead you wrong. Ladies this is for you to; if you are single, you need to realize that God has someone for you, but He is not about to give you someone according to your standards.

It's not about you; it's about the kind of life that He desires for you to have, with a spouse in your life.

The reason some of you are still single; is because God has to work on you, He has to get you ready to receive who He has for you, so be patient, and be still before Him.

There are a lot of things that make a marriage; it is not all just love and being loved, if that were the case no one would be married.

God has put you in a position of leadership even in finding a wife; and from this will come more leadership as the two of you join together in holy matrimony.

The woman is to submit to her husband as the man submits to the Lord.

Man of God, you are to treat her as your queen, Woman of God; he shall be your king. The woman that God has for you will make you proud of her, (Proverbs 31:11-12). You are to put no one, or anything before each other, only God; He should always be first.

If you follow His Word, and live by it daily, you will make it until the Lord calls the both of you home.

I celebrate those Christian men and women, who are living according to God's holy will, Amen.

# You Have Been Divinely Appointed

(Judges 14:4)

Used for His purpose

Every Christian has been divinely appointed to accomplish something in the name of Jesus.

But it will never get done if you are still running your life.

What are you connected to, or who? If you are born again you should be somewhere in the house of God, doing something in His Name.

God cannot use you sitting at home doing your own thing and thinking that you are pleasing Him; you are not (Hebrews 10:25).

Samson was a great man in power, but he was not that godly, even though he came from a godly home with godly parents. Samson had his mind set on having what he wanted.

Little did his parents know that it was the will of God?

Jews did not intermarry with other races, because it was against their law; the Philistines were not a circumcised people; his parents put this before him, but it did not work.

Sometimes we have to step back and let God have His way in the lives of our children, as did Samson's parents.

We will never be pleased at how some of them turn out, but there is nothing that you can do once they reach adulthood, but pray for them; they have the right to make their own choices, good or bad.

I know that we don't like everything that they do, and I am pretty sure that they do not like everything that we do.

God was using Samson to get to the Philistines, he had the Spirit of God, yet he still made wrong decisions, (Judges 3:25); whom is God trying to use you to get to? Are you a willing vessel? God will step in and let you know that He is God, when He says no, He means no; and when He tells us to go, then we are to go.

God can, and He will use your weakness for His own purpose. Samson only saw beauty in this woman as most men do; he never thought about her character.

Don't be fooled by the outer shell of a man or a woman. It will surely be you who will suffer the consequences. You cannot allow this flesh man to rule and lead; fleshly desires will get you into a lot of trouble.

We must follow the Holy Ghost because He leads us into all truth.

How many times have you made the mistake of doing something that was not good for you, and was not at all in your best interest? "Countless times" but He still "loves you" and "forgives you", every time.

Our bodies no longer belong to us; so when God calls you, answer; and be willing, to do what He is calling you to do. You may not know what it is that He wants you to do, but ask, Lord what is your will for my life, I assure you He will answer. A word of caution: it is not good to get everything you want.

*Scattered Thoughts*

# Family Reunion

(Genesis 42:7-8; Psalm 133:1-3)

A Description of what it's like

Everyone has to give an account of their wrongful doings somewhere down the road it is going to catch up with you.

Joseph has become a great leader in Egypt; he has been given authority over the surrounding lands.

This land included the land of his Father; his brothers have come to Egypt to buy supplies in order to make it through the famine that has come upon the land.

God's plan is always a perfect one, even though Joseph could not understand at the time why his brothers chose to treat him the way they did, God knew, He sees the big picture. Here are his brothers now standing before him; Joseph gets smart and decides to do things his way, for whatever reason.

It just may have been because they did not even have an idea of who he was, but he certainly knew them.

There was a great change in his looks; he no longer looked like a Hebrew; he now looks like and dresses like an Egyptian.

I love this story because it lets us know that you have to be very careful about how you treat your family members, regardless of how they treat you... How do you feel about your family? How have you been treated by them through the years?

I am sure there are some of you who can say great, and there are some who cannot. Whatever your answer, just know that God sees what is happening to you and He is not going to let it go on forever.

There is a stopping point in time for all things; Joseph's life assures us of this.

An offended person should let those who have committed the offense know; and they should also be willing to forgive.

That is way too much baggage for you to carry around every day.

You will never be able to help anyone with that frame of mind.

You will never be able to accomplish the things that God has for you if you hold on to the hurt, let it go, and be healed in the name of Jesus.

Joseph let go of his hurt, and had love and compassion for his brothers and for his father, who thought him to be dead, all those years. Oh God, you are so awesome? He knows exactly when to move; and it is always on time. I close with this, how good it is for brothers and sisters to dwell together. Satan you have lost another battle, because what you meant for our bad, God means it for our Good; hallelujah, Amen.

## Great Men Of Service

(1 Peter 2:16)

Holy Temples

As Christians we are called to submit to every authority.

Even though we do not feel like everyone deserves it that does not matter, it is the Word of God.

To obey His Word is divine; we are to obey the powers that be, for no power exists, without the Lord, (Romans 13:1).

Peter talks about us as being holy temples in verse five of this chapter.

We are to obey civil laws, as well as we obey the Word of God.

The Holy Spirit will help you to do what you need to do.

Law enforcement does not have any problem doing what they have been called to do.

For those of you who do not know, yes they are called to these positions.

Who in his right mind would want to have the job that some of them have, unless God calls you to it?

They have a grave responsibility to the community, the state, as well as the nation.

We all have a responsibility to make sure that we do our part.

Some people act as if these people are not human, but they are, they have families who love them the same as yours loves you.

So do what you are supposed to do, to help keep things decent and in order.

When you live your life as a servant of God, it makes you feel good about yourself.

Let us pray for those who are servants of our Communities, State, Nation and even the World.

Then you will not have to live your life in fear, the reason is that prayer certainly does change things.

Yes, we are free because of Jesus Christ; but we still have an obligation as citizens of the United States to do our part in this world.

Honor God, and also honor those that are servants in the world; when you carry this out, you really are pleasing God.

# The Voice Of God

(Deuteronomy 4:36)

Hear Him

Our God from heaven above has made us to hear his voice; a lot of Christians often say they have never heard Him, but I assure you, that you really have.

He speaks to you each and every day, He speaks through the Pastor on Sunday and Wednesday; He speaks to you in the Sunday school classes, and He really is speaking to you when you read His holy Word, He speaks to you when go into prayer and meditation.

The problem is, that you are refusing hear and obey.

He spoke to Moses, Joshua, David, the Hebrew boys, Daniel in the lions' den, Peter, John, Mary, Paul, and on and on; and He is speaking to you even now! Yes He is, and He is still giving direction to those that are His those that will hear and obey.

The question is, are you truly His? I believe that you are! But, you have got a lot of growing to do in Jesus.

You can never make a mistake as to what God is trying to do and say, through you; and with you, especially when you are tuned in wholeheartedly to Him.

How do you tune in? Glad you ask!

There is only one way, and it is to be spiritually minded; you cannot go to the Father in your flesh.

"God is a Spirit" and those that worship Him, <u>must</u> worship Him in spirit and in truth. There is no getting around this, because His way is the way.

Can you imagine where this world would be if we would be obedient to His Word. He is the One who gives us instructions…can't you hear Him calling out to you?

Even though you are looking at someone else standing in front of you talking, look past the individual, and see Him.

He's so real, so loving, and so worthy, He is to be obeyed and followed in every area of your life, not just some areas. So why not do it today? Follow Him; ask yourself, what is it, or who is it, that is keeping you from following the Lord? Only you would know.

## What Would Be Your *Proper Place*?

(St. Matthew 10:24; St. John 13:16-17)

Find It

We all know how important it is for some to have high positions, whether it is in the church or in the world.

But in reading this one scripture, I have found that we are all to be followers in one way or another, followers of someone else that is in leadership, we are not to just follow ourselves.

How can I put myself above the person that the Lord has called to rule over me?

Yet we see this happening in the churches, in the home, and in the work place.

God has called us all to be disciples; I have never seen where they (disciples) went above the one that was teaching them.

They always went back for instruction from the Master - Teacher, (Jesus Christ).

How awesome, it is a great thing to have this kind of obedience; this can only come by knowing the Word of God, and by living it.

I am convinced that this makes for a great leader. A disciple is simply a servant to the leader - teacher. A servant can never be higher than his master.

I realize as a human being there are things that you will not like, definitely the things that are mentioned above. But, think about it, God Our Father will be filled with joy, because you are doing what is right, and pleasing in His sight. You do this by staying in your proper place.

Maybe this is a part of the problem; a lot of Christians do not know exactly where their proper place is, this is why Christians are everywhere but where they should be. A good place to start would be a Bible based church that believes and teaches the unadulterated Word of Almighty God.

Tell the pastor your concerns, and he will direct you to where you should be. There is nothing greater than understanding; it keeps down a lot of confusion.

By following protocol a lot more will get done, and it will be done correctly.

I have always believed that as a disciple we should follow our leaders, there will be a time of releasing, and then you will be able to do the work that the Lord God has planted within you, and you will do it with an awareness of the fact that it is not about you but that it is all about Jesus, and Kingdom building. All of this comes with trust, if you cannot trust those that are over you, then you are probably in the wrong place, the wrong house. Trust is a very important factor in the life of a Christian. Finding your place will not be hard, if you trust Jesus as He places you where He would have you to grow, and then grow; you definitely will.

## Confinement
(1 Kings 2:36-37)

It could be you

This Word is very interesting, you see, this man had become a prisoner in his own home, and he was a dangerous person.

Solomon had given orders as to how he was to live, and what he should not do.

There are people today who are going through this very same thing.

They don't have to be considered bad, but they have become prisoners in their own homes.

They are afraid to venture out, and those that do; won't go far from home.

This is awfully sad, because God has given us this big beautiful world to live in; and some will never see it for what it really is.

There are some who have conditions that cause them to never leave home, some are obese, and cannot because they are unable to move on their own.

Some are imprisoned, because of something that they have done in society, so they have been given this punishment of wearing this lovely bracelet on their leg, you do know what I mean, in case some of you don't, house arrest.

There are many reasons one can be shut up in their home.

We have a lot of seniors that have reached a ripe and beautiful age, who are just not able to get out and go; the way that they desire to do.

What are you doing as a Christian to help them?

A lot of people are just looking; and going, not caring about anyone but himself or herself.

Please realize that there is a day coming in your life when you may be unable to go out on your own.

There are Christians who are confined to their homes; they are battling with cancer and different kinds of dreadful diseases, diseases that will not allow them to do anything at all. There are also others who have to go through this battle alone.

Don't you think for one minute that there is satisfaction in this for them because it certainly is not? Some of them do have family, but where are they? Some of them have a church family, but where are they?

If you know anyone who is going through this, pray for him or her, visit him or her, call him or her, send him or her a card. They will be grateful to hear from you; and you dear heart, will be glad that you did. Word to remember, "Your strength exists in what you do, and it certainly does come from within".

## Spiritual Adultery

(Jeremiah 3:1)

What life is it?

The Word of the Lord! Who will argue with that? When we were young and growing up there were a lot of things that we were not allowed to see or hear, and, you would get your head knocked off if you tried. My mother had a saying that some people would argue with a signboard!

I did not understand what she meant then, but I certainly do now.

Have you ever been there? In that place where you saw everybody's wrong but your own. Well, today God is giving you a chance to see yourself; you are not as pure as you think that you are.

I don't believe that there is a person on this earth that does not fit in this category (spiritual adultery).

Somewhere down this road of life you have stepped to the left; and you have gotten off of the street called straight.

I don't care how holy you say you are, or think that you are, you have fallen.

I am sure there are some who are going to be upset when they read this, well that means that you are being helped. You see, the Word of God is just what it professes to be, the Word of God; and The Truth, (who is Jesus Christ) will make you free, (St. John 8:32).

So be free today, my brothers and my sisters; and understand that game time is over. You have played long enough. You should be very tired at this point in your life of pretending about your feelings anyway, let the Lord teach you, in His Word, how to be a spiritual person.

God loves realness and rightness; that is what excites Him.

We have a Father who sits high and looks low; and, He knows everything there is to know about you, and me.

Jeremiah was a messenger to his generation, as stubborn as they were; and so it is today. God has many messengers, if you are in church, your pastor is your messenger, (angel of the house), are you hearing him? We have many who proclaim the Word of God; and yet the people go about their everyday routine as if it was nothing. People refuse to believe that God is going to punish the wicked for their evil deeds, but He is.

People also refuse to believe in Him for their eternal soul salvation; therefore they are on their way to an eternal hell.

What will it take people of God, for you to get to that place, where He desires you to be?

You cannot straddle the fence; that is ludicrous thinking on your part, you are like a crazy person in your thoughts.

He has given us the gift of discernment; and with that, you are able to determine if what you are hearing is sound doctrine. The Lord will never lead you wrong.

## They Say

(1 Samuel 8:7)

God said it

Have you ever wondered where the statement they say comes from; well it started with God. Nothing that we say or do is new under the sun.

Moses predicted that one day the Children of Israel would have a King over them (Deuteronomy 17:14-20).

God is talking with Samuel and has given him instruction to go to the people and let them know they do not need what they are asking for, which was a king.

Samuel warns the people of their wrong doings; and their wrong motives.

The people did not need a king because they had Jehovah; He was their King.

There are times when God will let you have your way; this was one of those times.

We to have often gotten our way; even when we knew that we shouldn't have, it may have been through your husband, friend, father, mother, sister, brother, fiancé, whoever or whatever, you still got your way.

We even go to God in prayer for things that we know we should not!

There are some who pray for harm to come to others. But I thank God that He does not answer those evil prayers.

Isn't it wonderful that we have a God who loves us so much, that sometimes He will, and does honor your request?

Our motives should always be pure and right, because God cannot use you when you have not submitted your life to Him, and He will not force you to change; that is totally up to you.

The people had become stubborn and stiff-necked, don't judge them, it is still alive today!

Don't you take it personal when you run into what they said, it's not against you; it is against the Lord God Almighty.

When we demand what we want from whomever God has sent, or we are disobedient to the one that is in leadership over us, then we reject God, not man.

I believe that if we would really look at it in the light of His Word; that we would without a shadow of a doubt turn back to the True and Living God, He is all that you will ever need.

You see, what you are saying does not really matter, if it does not line up with the Word of God, and His will. If you would be real and truthful about what you think you want, you would realize that you really don't know, and that is why God is here for you, and He knows exactly what is best for your life.

# A Three-Fold Cord

(Ecclesiastes 4:12)

Strength

Don't let greed get the best of you, if this is you, you may be up now, but you will not be always.

There are always going to be storms in our lives, and when the storm comes you will need someone to depend on.

There are those who are financially stable right now, and they feel that they do not need the help of anyone else, wrong answer, yes you do; everybody needs somebody on this road called life.

Solomon confirms it, we all need someone,

You may be single, but you need someone in your life to be accountable to. Yes, we all need that someone who will tap us on our shoulders, and let us have it, the real truth that is, and to bring us back in line with the will of God.

We should be grateful to God to have others in our lives who love us and do not mind letting us know when we are getting off the right path.

If you are a Christian you definitely need someone other than you, because most of the time you are never able to see where you are wrong.

Most Christians do have friends that they can depend on; but some do not.

There are a lot of people who come and go in your life; these people were not your friends.

Then there are those that you are around, those who do not have your best interest at heart, you have to realize this, and accept it as a fact.

Don't be so quick to think that everyone loves you, or for that matter cares about you, because they don't.

If you, on the other hand really care about whom you have befriended, you will help them, you will be concerned for them and about them.

Do you have friends who are in need but you never reach out to them? What about your church family friends? After all that is where a lot of friendships occur, in the church.

When we as Christians go through things together it brings us closer to one another; it makes things better; to know that you are not alone. It also pleases God, and this brothers and sisters makes for a strong cord, that nothing can penetrate, and the glory belongs to God, Amen.

## A Broken Spirit

(Proverbs 17:22)

Man without God

This speaks of the inner man, your outer life and your well- being has a lot to do with what goes on inside of you.

A lot of Christians today are dealing with this very thing; they are hurting on the inside and pretending to be glad on the outside. They are depressed, disgusted, and devastated at where they are, and what they have become.

You have got to get to that place spiritually, where you do not let the devil rule in your life, because you do not belong to him.

So why are you still over there playing games with him and his imps? It is time for you to come out of the darkness into God's marvelous light.

This stuff will eventually take you out, so get where you are supposed to be.

A sad spirit always finds its way to the outside, in other words it shows.

If you are a happy person on the inside, then your happiness is going to show; but if you are sad the same thing, people will know.

Your countenance looks like what's on the inside of you, (it transitions from the inside to the outside).

If you are always sorrowful and sad it weakens you, things will change in your body; and it will not be for the better, it will break you down from the inside as it makes it's way to the outside.

Even smiling makes a difference in how you feel, try it. If you are feeling sad and don't want to smile just let your jaws and mouth move into that position anyway. I guarantee you this will work; it sets off the good things on the inside of the body.

Isn't that wonderful, you are not really trying, but you find that you are definitely helping yourself.

There is another way you can help your body!

Whatever it is that you are allowing to hold you hostage, just let it go, ask the Lord to help you, and He will.

The Holy Ghost is right there inside of you, He is just waiting on you to let Him have His way in your life, you will be glad that you did; this is where your "Joy" will come, so choose today to live your life God's way; because His way is the way, the best and only way.

## The Promise Of Forgiveness

(Psalms 103:12)

He forgives and He moves our sins

We should be grateful to the Lord for His loving forgiveness; there is nobody else who can do what Jesus has done for us.

And, still, He is the one who is denied daily by mankind.

I thank God that He has given us this promise in His Son, who died on the cross at Calvary, and took all of our sins to that old rugged cross with Him.

We should be truly grateful that He does not hold our sins against us, nor does He accuse us of them, as a matter of fact He forgets them, all because of Jesus.

He is a God who is slow to anger; He is nothing like us, because we are easily angered; and we love to hold what someone does to us, against them forever.

But as Christians, we are to become more like Jesus; we can only do this by studying His Word, by going before the Lord in prayer, and in meditation.

The Lord separates our sins from us by forgiving us of them; it has already been done,

He did it over two thousand years ago, and it does not require repeating, Hallelujah.

As Christians we are to do the same by those who transgress against us.

He shows us His mercy in everything He does, (Hebrews 8:12) and we know, that His mercy, endures forever.

Jesus Christ is our mercy; He is our compassion, He is all we will ever need.

If you are remembering a sin that you have committed, then it is on you, because it is far from the Father; that is His Word.

He is not just speaking about sin, it is about forgiveness too.

When God says something, He does it; and He keeps His promises.

If He is your Lord and Savior, then you share in this joy.

The joy of knowing that whatever I do in this body, He has already forgiven, and wiped it out, now that is joy. Include yourself here if you are a born again saint, then give thanks to the Lord for all that He has done for you! Shout it to the rooftops.

## Will You Ever Learn?

(2 Timothy 3:7)

Not knowing

It's a sad thing to be spiritually illiterate to be led by falseness (false prophets).

People who choose not to get into the Word of God (the Bible) can wind up in a world of trouble.

It is happening every day, there are people, who are saved, but they are too lazy to read His Word. Therefore they are falling into all kinds of false beliefs because they will not go into the Word for themselves.

There comes a time when you have to read, and study for yourself; don't always depend on a man or woman to get you to where God is calling you too.

When you are more carnally minded, than spiritual minded; there will always be something very wrong with your faith.

There are people in this world who see right through you, and they also know what they can do to you, and with you.

They know that you are vulnerable, and that they can have their way in your life.

But, when you know the Word for yourself, you make it impossible for a person to pull you out of the fold.

The Word will make you bold, it will help you stand, and it will help you when you speak.

There is no way that you can do this if there is no Word inside of you; it is imperative that you read and study. It is not enough to have the Lord around you; you need His Spirit (Holy Ghost), inside of you.

When the Holy Ghost is seated in His proper place, nothing and I do mean nothing, can get to you.

You have to be in a positive position led by "The Holy Ghost", to acknowledge the truth when you hear it.

Now, if you are open to learning, and it is my prayer that you are; join a Bible believing church, where you can grow, and then you will be a great asset to your Father who is in heaven. You see, someone needs you to show him or her the way.

## The Light
(John 12:43)

They chose

Who is your light and who is it that you praise? Who is it that you have chosen to follow? We see things happening in the news, on the Internet and on our jobs, and etc.

People are putting men before God; the one who gave His only Son for them.

They have forgotten Him and have abandoned Him they have turned to the ways of the world.

The Word of God tells us to be transformed, and not to conform, (Romans 12:2).

There are many people who believe in the Lord, but they do not want to come down off of their high horse and give Him the glory and honor that He deserves.

There is no one, or anything, that should take the place of Jesus.

All that evil does is, it keeps you in the dark; evil comes from our archenemy, Satan.

Jesus knew that there would be those who would profess to love Him, but would turn on Him for the things of this world.

Change is in order, you have been saved, and it is a part of the process.

It does not matter how much you have, or what you stand to lose; you must change. Come back to the Light of Jesus Christ, He shines; and His Light will never go out.

His Light is not as the light of man.

People who have a lot of money, and things are less likely to give up what they have verses people who do not have.

The crazy thing about it is, that it all belongs to the Lord; He is the one who has allowed you to have what you have, and to do what you do.

Why should you praise Him? You should Praise Him because He is LORD, and for no other reason. He deserves your praise, and it should not be a hard thing for you to do, if you believe in Jesus, yes you should and must confess Him, to everyone that you come in contact with.

Somebody needs to know, that you know, who Jesus is; could it be that their life (eternal) is depending on you; yes, Jesus is the Light of the world; now praise, honor, and glorify Him, forever.

# The Christian Minister

(1 Peter 4:11)

Who?

Jesus Christ should always get the credit for what you do as a servant of the Lord.

Peter mentions the speaking minister (pastor/preacher) as well as the ministering minister (deacon/servant).

If you speak, let it be as the oracles of God. God is still giving His Word to people in prophecy today; ministers are now coming forth and speaking boldly what they hear. It's like a wild fire spreading in the house of the Lord.

Jesus say's that we, who are servants, let it be in the strength of the Lord.

We can do nothing in our own strength; it all comes from allowing the Holy Ghost to have His way in our lives.

In our own strength we get tired, we give out, and we give up.

Why do you do what you do? Do you do it because you love the Lord? We must be committed to loving and serving one another. Then we will be endowed with the power to bring in those that are lost.

Peter also informs us of the fact that the time is not long; Jesus Christ is coming back again.

We do not need to turn back, but we do need to keep walking straight ahead.

We need to keep our minds stayed on Him; we need to be concerned about our fellowman; and we need to stay constant in prayer.

We also need to thank God for allowing us to be a part of such a great harvest, the harvest of bringing in the sheaves, (lost souls).

It takes all of us to do Kingdom work, it's not about one or two people, it's about all of us pulling together and making sure that we do what is pleasing in the sight of the Lord. This dear one is what is most important, that His will be done in you, and in me.

## Music Creates A Memory

(2 Chronicles 5:13; Ecclesiastes 2:8b; St. Luke 15:25)

Oh my Lord

We cannot remember what the pastor's sermon was on Sunday morning, but we can remember songs, and the music that comes with it from years past.

For example: as youth most of us were raised on Jesus loves me, Amazing Grace, and Precious Lord, just to name a few.

As we grew older and were able to do things under our own power we went for it.

All those things that we wanted to do, that is. We started going to clubs and honkey tonks as some have called them.

You enjoyed every minute, every second, and every day, that you were in the world, and, I remind you, that these are saved people. You danced, you sang, and you fell in love.

You did things that you should not have done, even though you had been taught the right way of doing things. When you finished doing what you did best, you would ask God to forgive you, and then; you would turn around and do it all over again, oh yes you did.

If I were in a position to ask you some questions now, and you were able to answer; in reference to what you were listening to in the sixty's; I am sure you could give me some quick answers? If I said well, what about the seventy's, the eighty's, and on and on, I know you could give me an answer. How do I know? I know because that is what each generation has been moved by down through the years, music, and we are still being moved by it even today. We shout too it, we dance to it in the church, and out of the church.

You even got in trouble from listening to it, because certain songs would take your mind, and they would have you thinking in ways that you should not have been thinking and doing things that you should not have been doing, (cheating and you know).

Even in the Bible days music played a big part in the way people acted.

Even the Devil knows this; because he knows the Word, and he uses it against man more than he does anything else, think about it.

This is how he tries to trap people and keep them from coming to Christ.

There are Christian's who will tell you, I am not through with the blues; they still venture out to hear it, and they still play it. The same goes for the younger generation, they are still holding theirs to.

Look at the differences in the church, you have the children who can't get into what the older saints like; and you have the older saints who don't like what the youth like. I think when we come to our spiritual senses we will all get off of the like thing.

Because it is not about what you like, or what they like it is about what it takes to bring the lost to Christ. The Holy Ghost is intelligent, and He does not need our help. If you have been caught up with the Lord and really want to please Him, you will see that all of it is good. After all He ordained it! (Psalm 150) tells us to make a joyful noise unto the Lord. When you were in your youth, you did your thing, now let the Holy Ghost do His, in the House, the church. It took you long enough to get here, so stop your complaining, and be a blessing.

## Just Look

(Psalm 34:5)

He is there

*Fresh Bread; if you look and keep looking you shall see me, I AM is here.*

God is an Awesome God.

Have you ever had Him speak something to you while you were asleep; or between sleep and woke?

If you are close to Him, you will hear Him and you will know that is Him who is speaking.

That is exactly what happened to me this lovely December morning 2006, I got up feeling good, with much excitement, when I heard these words in my inner self; God said, "If you look, and keep looking, you shall see me, I AM here".

This let me know that He is ever present in my life; I had been praying about something that I wanted the Lord God to do for our home, and I am telling you it is done!

God will do the same for you.

When God blesses us we must in return be a blessing; and I did.

We must come into His presence with glory, honor, and praise, and I did.

I know that He is taking me higher in my walk with Him, and I praise Him.

It is an honor and a privilege for me to be welcomed by my Father to do great things in His name.

I am not one who wants to live my life with no accomplishments; I must do my part in helping to build up the Kingdom of God. What about you?

I ask the Lord to let me do those things that I can; and do it in a great way, and not to do it for man to pat me on my back, but to do it so that "My God" always gets the glory.

I do, what I do, as unto the Lord, He is the one that is most important in my life.

I welcome every adventure that He brings my way, every challenge, even though they can be, and most of the time are a great struggle for me.

That is what makes us stronger in our faith walk; that is what keeps us on our spiritual toes, so you just keep looking, and you will see Him.

## Armor Bearer

(1 Kings 16:21; 2 Samuel 18:15)

From armor-bearer to King

You never know what God has in store for your life until you walk according to His holy will. David was Saul's armor-bearer.

David was obedient and did what he was told to do.

Even when Saul lost it, David was still there for him, now that is faithfulness.

David would have killed for Saul if the need had ever presented itself.

Here Saul loses it, and turns on David out of sheer jealously.

Don't you let jealously, keep you from serving where you have been called.

Pastors today have armor-bearers; I don't think that some of them realize what an honor it is to have this position.

An armor-bearer is appointed to his position at the discretion of the pastor; they are Christian-men who love the Lord, and the called man of God. They are also men who will be loyal, and protecting in any way that they can.

They are obedient to the Word of God, and they give, in the tithe and the offering.

They know the service that they are providing is holy, and they know that it is not for show.

God's Word gives us facts; an armor-bearer was a most dedicated worker. He would even give his life to the service of being a watchman over the Angel of the church, how awesome. Armor-bearers should be a physical and spiritual strength to their pastor, because there will be times when you will have to hold him up physically; because he loses strength to the preaching power of the Word. Concerning his spiritual needs, you are to always hold him up in prayer.

If you don't have a great respect for him (the Pastor); then do not desire this position.

Don't think just do, God will bless you, (David shows this by the way he treated Saul).

You should always be submissive to the powers that rule over you; as a matter of fact this is good for all Christians everywhere. If you are to serve him while he preaches or teaches do it as though you were serving "The Lord Jesus Himself". An armor-bearer should not want to be praised, or think that he is greater than whom he is serving, (the honor is in your serving). You may be the one that has been appointed (called) to take care of the little things, so do it faithfully and lovingly.

## Pay What You Owe

(Proverbs 3:27-28)

It is a must

This is something we as Christians have definitely got to start doing.

We owe people, and we act like it is nothing.

We can go for years doing this even though The Holy Ghost reminds us time after time. But, what do we do, we just keep on going as though we have not been reminded at all.

Well I can tell you this from my own experience; God gives us ample time to pay what we owe.

We say that we mean well, and we intend to get it done, God is saying; not good enough, He is watching our every move, just do it.

There are those who owe somebody right now and have for a long, long, time, now be honest with yourself, yes, it may be hard for you; but do it and then God can move in your life.

 (Proverbs 3:27) tells us not to withhold good from those who deserve it.

How is it that you are getting what you want, but not doing what you should?

Some Christians are guilty of this most of the time; they take advantage of others.

Keep it up; payday is coming, you do have to face God one day?

Why do you get joy out of having something that does not belong to you?

One true fact is this, that when you go to work, you expect to get paid for the work you have done; well, it is the same with those that you owe.

If you borrowed it, pay it back; if you had something done in good faith with the promise to pay, pay; (someone worked for you).

When people ask you to help them and you have it, but you still say no He is going to discipline you.

God has blessed us tremendously; as a matter of fact, He is the reason that you have what you possess now. His desire is that we help one another, pay what we owe, and live your life in a way that is pleasing in His sight; this is not too much to be asked of us by Our Father.

# The Big "O's"

(Genesis1: 1 - Revelation 22:21)

Our God

God really does have a sense of humor; this morning before I got up; I was thinking, and praying. I was also thinking about my next lesson title; when I heard Him say, the Big O's.

All I could do was smile in my spirit and think, *"My God How Great Thou Art"*.

You have to know for yourself that God really is an Awesome God!

He does not need mans help to do anything; but, because of the love that He has for us in behalf of His Son Jesus Christ, we have been afforded an opportunity to serve alongside Him.

Today I want to share the power of His name with you, after all, what good is it that He is your Father, and you don't know Him the way that you should. It is my prayer that after your reading this, that you would make getting to know your Father better a priority in your life.

The first *"O"* He is now and will always be, present in your life and in mine.

<u>*God is Omnipresence:*</u> This Word means "always present." Since God is infinite, He knows no boundaries. He is everywhere at the same time.

You will find this truth throughout the Bible, He says "I AM with you always" it is repeated in both the Old Testament and New Testament.

Jesus even said it, before Abraham was, I AM. This is assurance to all that will accept and believe in Him.

It was also an assurance to His disciples, knowing what they knew about Jesus made it easier for them to be witnesses to those that they would come in contact with.

It gives us a peace of mind that when we stand before those that are lost that we can do what we have been called to do, simply because we are instruments of His holy will.

He speaks through us to the lost, and the lost become saved.

This lets us know that He is also present with them, (Holy Ghost) giving them that opportunity to come out of the darkness into His marvelous light.

The second *"O"* He has all power, nothing can or will ever change it.

*God is Omnipotence:* This Word means "all powerful". Since God is infinite and since He possesses power, He possesses infinite power! God allows us to have limited power, our power that we possess will never amount to His, if you don't believe me check out Satan; he found out the hard way. "We will always get tired in our little power, but God never tires, He is ever moving ever on the go." We require rest, God does not; there are things that press on us, but we have to stop sometime because we are not made to just go and go.

The third *"O"* His knowledge is beyond anything that we could ever think or imagine; it cannot be reached.

*God is Omniscience:* This Word means, "all knowing". Our Father is perfection, He is Knowledge, He is Wisdom, He is the Book of Books, and He has no need of schools and teachers, as do we, He is the Master Teacher! (What could you teach an all-knowing God?) He is an Incredible God.

You cannot hide anything from Him, because before you even do it; He already knows. What a "Mighty God" we serve.

# I Found Him

(Psalm 105:4; Isaiah 55:6.)

The duty of man

Finding God is something that you must do for yourself even though we are led to

The Name of Jesus Christ and led to believe; it takes more.

There is a journey that man must take of his own accord; even before we come to know the Lord it pulls at us we are even taught as little children that God exists.

We are taught to say our prayers before we lay down to sleep, we are taught to say grace before we put food in our mouths or consume our drink.

Some people are saying that they do not know what it is, or who it is, but I differ with you.

Don't let the evil that is inside of you have rule in your life.

The Lord God has put Himself into the hearts and minds of every man on this earth.

You can call yourself whatever you desire to; but, you do know that God exists!

It is as plain as the nose on your face; you may not ever accept Him, but you definitely know of Him.

This makes for a sad testimony, that man would deny God, the Father and Creator of all life, and even sadder is the fact that your soul will be lost forever, throughout all eternity.

This word found is used quite often by Christians and none Christians concerning Christ. We like saying "I found the Lord" it is true that some have; and oh how sweet it is.

Could it be that God is not in your thoughts, well He should be, (Psalms 10:4)?

There are people who have problems with those that say they have found the Lord, well, get over it. When you are lost and come to Christ you have found the greatest treasure that man will ever come to know in his lifetime; and the life to come.

You also have the Word of God before you in Scripture today that testifies to this very fact; He says, seek; so that requires something on your part.

How do you seek Him? You do it in your prayer life, each and every day.

Could this be reason that you have not found Him for yourself?

Not only are we to seek Him, but also we are to call upon His holy name.

A Name that is so "Awesome" you can speak and be saved; (Jesus), you can speak it and be delivered, (Jesus), and you can speak it and be healed, (Jesus).

These are just some of the things that speaking the Name of Jesus will do for you. God does welcome the wicked, but the wicked has to change their ways in order to receive His grace and His mercy.

It does not matter who you are, or how much you possess, you have got to change, or you will be lost forever.

## What Are You Speaking?

(Proverbs 18: 4)

Good or bad

Words can be helpful, loving, and caring; or they can be very hurtful, even destructive down to the very bone of a man. It is very important that we watch our speech.

People really don't care about what they say or who they say it to. It seems as though respect just got thrown right out of the window.

Have you ever paid attention to the songs that are being sung in the world today?

Some of the words that people are saying are coming forth out of madness and anger; and they are not nice at all.

Bad words are like bad water, they run deep, and the flow is not good, it stinks (stagnate). You don't have to say a profanity to have said something bad, even though it does make it worse; people say bad things everyday concerning others.

They don't have to see anything, they just make things up, to put it another way, and they lie.

They don't have any business, so they will make you their business.

These people are not all sinners; some of them are Christians, who have not come into the fullness of Christ and His love for them within. Because when they do, they will cease to do these kinds of things.

There are a lot of things that need to be accomplished concerning the growth of the Kingdom of God, but it will not and cannot get done unless people change.

The Word of God plainly states that you are a fool!

That should be enough to cure you, even though it probably will not!

It is a bad reflection on you, when you are a child of God and you can sit up in conversation with others and say bad things about your brothers or sisters in Christ.

I caution you, to remember, that you will certainly reap what you sow, (that is a promise from the Lord). A person of wisdom can know things and not use it to hurt others. What they will do because of the love in their heart, and the love that they have for Jesus Christ; is become a protector, of whomever the others are talking about.

Have you ever been lied on, how did you feel? Have you ever lied on someone else?

Be the wise one and spread words of love and encouragement.

People enjoy being around a wise and caring person, but a liar leaves a lot to be desired. Read the Proverbs and grow, there is a lot of Wisdom within its pages.

Take yourself into the Word, and the Lord God will speak to you. Believe me, there is nothing like hearing the voice of God, absolutely nothing, and secondly, there is nothing like obeying what He is saying to you.

# Faith Based On Experience

(2 Timothy 3:15)

That is not faith

If you are basing your faith on what you think and feel, that is not faith!

Faith is hoping, trusting, and believing in that which you cannot see.

You cannot trust your flesh, because the flesh is sinful; it will never, on its own, do what is right.

You may be going through today, and your faith can help to make a world of difference.

The Word of God tells us that when we are weak, then we are strong,

(2 Corinthians 12:10).

If you have been born again let the Holy Ghost rule, no, it won't be easy; but it gets better with each day, learning how to live in His Spirit.

This is a problem for a lot of Christians; but you do have to let go and let God.

You cannot profess to be saved and not let it show.

You are living in a world that is full of unbelievers, and they need to be able to look at those that are saved and say; if he or she made it I can also.

God did not create you to be a weak being, nor did He create you to always be totally dependent on others.

You have got to transition to that place where He can use you for the Salvation of another.

It is past the time of feeling sorry for yourself and laying around in those sorrows doing nothing.

Get up, and get going, in The Name of Jesus Christ, Our Lord.

It does not matter what your age; the Master can use you.

People are dying every day because of lack of knowledge; they are falling to the tricks of the enemy (Satan), what a waste. Let us be prayerful and caring for those that are around us because their very life may just depend on you.

## Every Where You Go He Has Already Been

(Hebrews 4:15)

Aren't you glad?

Jesus Christ is our Awesome Savior and Deliverer; there is nothing that we have been through that He has not been through.

There is nowhere we can go that He has not already been.

There is no temptation that comes to us that He has not already conquered.

This is very encouraging for me, and I pray that it is for you also.

I have to keep this very plain, so that you will understand; even though Jesus went through when He was in His flesh, He never sinned.

He lived and breathed the same as you and I, He lived as a man who had to face the world daily, and its troubles; and again I tell you, He never sinned.

He could feel like we feel, He hurt from things said about Him the same as we do; He felt pain in His body the same as we do.

But, I say to you again, He never sinned.

We, on the other hand, cannot say this, because we do sin each and every day.

It matters not how holy you are, you have sinned.

It may be a tough pill to swallow, but you will be better for it.

Jesus Christ, who are our blessed Lord and Savior has given us a way back to the Father.

He has afforded to us the greatest gift that a man could ever receive, no matter what your season.

He has much sympathy, and love for those who will come back to Him.

He is the sinless Savior.

He is the Savior of the World.

He is God Incarnate.

He is whatever you want Him to be in your life.

So you be very sure, that in the process of all this that you are His.

## About the Author

A devoted wife, mother of 5, grandmother of 10, and great grandmother of 4. Oregean Adams, lovingly known by most as "Jean", is known for her wisdom, grace, and love of the Word of God. She is a native of Brinkley, Arkansas and relocated to the Little Rock area as a teenager.

Jean is loved by many for her honest and genuine personality. She takes pleasure in using her life lessons to be an example and beacon of light for any and every one she comes in contact with. At the age of 16, she lost her mother. This death was followed by her father at the age of 24 and her daughter at 31. These life tragedies alone are an example of some of the hurdles she has had to endure and overcome early in life and part of her passion to help others.

She received an online certification from Charles Stanley School of Ministry in the Fall of 2005. In April 2012, she received a certificate of Completion in "Building the Foundation Courses" and "Strengthening the Foundation Ministry Electives" from the St. Luke School of Ministry. Jean is currently an active member of St. Luke Missionary Baptist Church in Jacksonville, Arkansas. Here, under the leadership of Pastor Eric L. Alexander, she has been a member for 20 plus years. She serves as a Minister, Christian Life Development Teacher, and a member of The Voices of St. Luke.

It is her prayer and desire that *Scattered Thoughts* will serve as a resource for Christians to grow in their one-on-

one time and that any non-believer that reads it and develop a relationship with Christ.

# *Word Angels*

## An Imprint of
### *Butterfly Typeface Publishing*

Iris M. Williams
PO Box 56193
Little Rock AR 72215

(501) 823 – 0574

info@butterflytypeface.com

www.butterflytypeface.com

www.ingramcontent.com/pod-product-compliance
Lightning Source LLC
Chambersburg PA
CBHW050120170426
43197CB00011B/1656